DRIVING YOURSELF
OUT OF DEBT

DRIVING YOURSELF
OUT OF DEBT

Steve Sloan

authorHOUSE®

AuthorHouse™
1663 Liberty Drive
Bloomington, IN 47403
www.authorhouse.com
Phone: 1-800-839-8640

First published by AuthorHouse 09/30/2011

ISBN: 978-1-4670-3139-4 (sc)
ISBN: 978-1-4670-3138-7 (ebk)

Library of Congress Control Number: 2011916801

Printed in the United States of America

Any people depicted in stock imagery provided by Thinkstock are models, and such images are being used for illustrative purposes only.
Certain stock imagery © Thinkstock.

This book is printed on acid-free paper.

CONTENTS

PREFACE

Getting out of debt invades the mind of every human being at one time or another. We look for excuses as to why we get into debt in the first place but in reality we live in a society that allows us to be anything at any time and we often choose to be anything at anytime. We turn our heads at those hungry and those in need or not as clever or intellectual as we are to fulfill our own selfish desires and we even use others weaknesses to entice our own gain. It's a dog-eat-dog world and we have power when we have money. Or is it so important that we look like we have money? Each day proves to be an economic down fall but when it comes to our personal financial achievements we use our tunnel vision to make reality disappear on the sidelines. The reality of debt ever lingers in the background of our peripheral vision and haunts us when we go to sleep. It makes us happy and said, evil and mad, it even caresses the façade of our own dreams. It puts us in places we've never thought of being and it takes away all that we've ever been.

Getting out of debt takes something we were never taught by our parents. A subject school never offered. The decision to get out of debt takes a different type of human being. A human being willing to acknowledge that something may be wrong with the way he lives his lifestyle. That he may have made a mistake along the way. That, maybe what you see is what you get is not exactly the status quote. But to step back and even look at ones self is an advantage far above most people who wish they could succeed in life.

Yet it is possible. Through the realization that you need help and that the first acknowledgement must be made by you; the reality that something can and should be done to free yourself from the beast of burden, that monster called debt.

This book explains how to make the transition to a new way of living; a way that very few decide to travel, a way to do something unheard of as the American way of life. This book does in fact suggest, a last ditch effort to pay off your debts while living out of your car using your existing living expenses as a means of income.

When you read this book seriously consider the consequences and dangers involved in its application. This author started out documenting a process to calculate a way to expel the irony of debt but ended up documenting, in come circumstances, life and death situations directly effecting him.

The moral of the premises of this book is to acknowledge that accomplishment can be made if you are willing to sacrifice and remember where you came from so you don't make the same mistakes over and over again.

ABOUT THE AUTHOR

Steven Eric Sloan: born and raised in the City of Pasadena California. Married to Cynthia Ann Sloan, and now residing in Fontana, CA. Steve is retired from the Los Angeles Police Department as an Audio Visual Technician and Cindy works in Child Services. When Steve is not working with wires bulbs and props he is helping Cindy understand the aspects of Video Photography and together they are learning how to cope with the aspirations of building there own world in the field of Creative Arts. Very much in love, God walks them through adventurous weekends and unintentional missions to great experiences in life and things to talk about. Collecting each journey on tape with the equipment they have accumulated over the years supports their vision of building an establishment for people to come and be entertained in a unique manner. They want to build a venue of Christian entertainment. A place free from the distractions of religion and replace that with relationship.

Steve's writing career started in 1985, while unemployed after a divorce and walking out on his then three-year-old daughter. Moving back to Pasadena, he was star struck by how easy it was to get caught up in the bright lights and glimmer of Hollywood and those who quickly seek you out to steal from you, your dream as long as you have a dollar to spare. Curious about making movies and having something on his heart he wanted to say about his life,

Steve researched the aspect of how to write his own screenplay. Over the next six to nine months, living under the roof of his mother, at the age of thirty-one Steve completed his first feature film "The Ultimate Goal" where he includes his life's experiences trying to start a new career after being laid off from jobs and having no where to turn but home. One Hundred or so scripts later he has decided to try his hand at a book. "Driving Yourself Out Of Debt" is just one facet of his life's experience as he relays to you a u-turn in life and his master plan to be free from debt in a fashion most people may cringe at, using himself as the tangible element to set the pace.

AUTHOR'S ACKNOWLEDGEMENTS

To my wife Cynthia and friend Joanne Lett-Sellers, thanks for still wanting to be a part of my life after finding out what I use to be and what I'm constantly evolving into. Thank you for keeping me thinking I'm still a normal person and that I'm not the first human being to go through such endeavors from all the mistakes I've made in life.

Also, to my wife Cynthia, I just can't believe that it's just happen stance—you coming into my life. God knew what I needed to make it through this unique drivers training course. Though "Driving Yourself Out of Debt" was conceived without you, you allowed me to use your nature to give it birth. I am truly blessed to have such a great woman; these pages are brighter because of you.

To my children and other family members, who don't know me very well or at all, there are very few words spoken in this adventure where I didn't at least take the time to stop and pray for you. So many incidences sparked a memory of you for me to dwell upon. For whatever reason this time is lost without you maybe these pages will help you to understand the man you never knew or at least the man who is just here for now. Just know—I never meant to hurt you and only God knows whatever pain I've cause you is well vindicated by the pain in my heart living without your love.

Finally, to you! To whom I may never know or say hello to on the streets. We pass each other everyday. We spend our money in the same world. We touch one another through each dollar we spend. You send a message through each giving it becomes a form of communication to one another. I'll pay your interest you pay my principle. We are connected you know. We may not know each other by name but we all depend on the same faces, on the currency we share.

FORWARD
by
Cynthia Sloan

The awesome thing about the book 'Driving Yourself Out Of Debt' is that the author, Steve Sloan, literally lives, in his car while driving toward freedom from the clutches of debt. Steve penned his day-to-day experiences living virtually homeless, and thus the book 'Driving Yourself Out Of Debt'.

When I meant Steve, I was so impressed by the way he spoke so openly about his purpose for living in his car. He said paying rent was not in his budget and some sacrifices are always made when someone sets out to obtain any worthwhile goal. Getting out of debt was his. Steve felt strongly about paying back what he owed, and when I suggested filing bankruptcy, he said 'filing bankruptcy is not an option, it is not something I believe in.'

As for me, about six years ago my computer business was folding and I maxed out all of my credit cards refusing to let it go. Ultimately, I lost the business and found myself in great debt, which followed me for years. One day Steve was over visiting, and as I walked in the living room I found him sitting on the floor with notebook and pin in hand and various piles of bills spread across the floor.

I was so impressed, right then and there I asked him to help me get out of debt. He did just that . . . and you know what? I didn't have to start living in my car.

ABOUT THIS BOOK

The rich keep it a secret about how to get rich, unless of course you pay them to toss you a few tid-bits of information in which case they call it a seminar. Even then there is always something left out the most important part, until you pay them to tell you the secret to success, which, somehow never works for you. One famous author said "If you want to get out of debt you have to spend less than you make over a long period of time" 'Rich Dad Poor Dad' By Robert Kiosaki.

This book 'Driving Yourself Out of Debt' is not necessarily for those who want to get rich but for those contemplating robbery or suicide because you are over your head in debt. Just look to the left or right of the section where this book will be resting. Behold, hundreds of people are talking about it—MONEY! They make it sound so easy—spend like this, save like that. Invest what you have, don't invest. Give, give, give; you can't afford not to give. But what if you don't have anything to spend, what if you don't have anything to save or GIVE? There is hope, there always is. In this book you will not see how I got rich because I'm not rich and quite frankly have done a little investigation and found what wealth can do to you negatively. I'm not an expert speaker by any means and the only thing I have going for me is life experiences.

I'm going to relay that experience to you in hopes that I can offer some comfort to the stress of living and thinking there is no hope of getting out of debt. I may not have the right answer for you and your situation may not apply but we all live under the same sun so that means we have something in common and the value of getting out of debt is worth it's weight in gold.

INTRODUCTION

Aha . . . the sound of rain drops splattering against my hood. What solitude, concealed by the condensation of my own breaths. I can see out, but they can't see in.

These moments are precious to me. Very few people experience the sights and sounds of life from this perspective. For some, it is out of necessity, for others a temporary inconvenience, and still some make this style of life a conscious choice.

This book is intended for those of you who are either already victim to an unforeseen event that has catapulted your life into a four-wheeled frontier. Or you've gone home to find your spouse has changed the locks on the doors only after charging all the credit cards to the max, as you hear party music going on inside.

Life is filled with surprises, and surprises are meant to catch you off guard, and when those surprises stem from economic challenges, very few people are prepared. That is the reason I am writing this book.

If you have found that the stress monster is using you as a pin cushion as an example to train his cohorts on how to successfully keep a good soul pinned down. Or you are bound and determined to release yourself from the progression of debt by any means necessary.

Then you are in possession of the right information. The key to unlock the door of captivity that's been keeping you hostage and confined to walls of self-destruction, frustration and even, in some cases a lack of true friendship.

A few words of caution: The physical application of this book is intended for the person who has the resources necessary to obtain or borrow a vehicle that has enough room in it to stretch out, is free from mechanical defects, registered and insured. It also requires that you own or at least have access to a computer with the Excel spreadsheet software installed and finally, a job, some continuous form of income no matter what the amount.

The practical aspects of this book are not recommended for the lone female or mothers with children. This book describes situations challenging to your protection let alone having to undertake the responsibility of watching out for others. Though the processes to be explained have proven successful for me, it will be under very specific conditions and circumstances that others may experience the same success. Never the less, every effort has been made to include the majority of conditions for those persons with a desire to obtain freedom from debt by encompassing one of the most awkward means necessary, creating a means of delivering yourself out of debt while living in your vehicle.

The person most likely to benefit from this book is a self sufficient adult, currently employed, with access to a vehicle which he or she may utilize freely. I cannot over stress the danger of following the suggestions offered in the following pages. Just listen to any television or radio station, the media spurts out information regarding those persons who watch the news one night and become the news the next.

Our current world order does not offer us the privilege to supersede the expectations of being considered average without being placed in the cross hairs of weapons of confrontation swaying in the hands of public ridicule. There are some who feel that if you're not as successful as they are, you are just sucking up air. Good air that they themselves could be using if only they could figure out a way to clog your nasals or cause you to suddenly malfunction. These people are crazy enough to take the matter in there own hands and by forcing you to give them your share of air taking you out themselves.

Living out of your car is nothing to shake a stick at. Yes, you can over come some great hurdles blocking your way to the finish line of financial freedom. But believe me, being the winner does not come without paying a price.

Through dedication, practice and a commitment to follow through with a predetermined plan, you can leap from one frying pan and steer clear of another.

I mentioned earlier that you could get out of debt by using the principles of how to live out of your car. How! You may ask?

Let me take you back, back to where it all began. Way before I began practicing the technical know how, if you notice any, on how to produce these writings.

CHAPTER 1

DRIVING TO INDEPENDENCE

I have always been a survivor, constantly looking for ways to improve myself, and the life I lead. Finding answers to any problem that may come my way. Now that may not sound so different than what you do on daily bases but after failing in most aspects of life and coming from a family that too often accepted a life of mediocre (and that's the worst okra there is) its difficult for a young man to learn to grow to be a first class citizen when he has no example of how to be a man.

My interest in success came early in life. But, then what is success? What does it mean to be successful? My research on this subject has proven that we humans have adapted many definitions describing the meaning of success. Some believe that success is wealth, money and lots of it. Some feel a promotion to a prominent position at your nine to five. To others, getting away with a crime, which for a period of time exhibits financial gain. What ever your definition may be, you will never reach your mark unless you first formulate a plan and then most importantly, stick to it.

Through my childhood I gained the gift of independence. Helping my mother raise my sister and brother I was quick to learn and understand the meaning of responsibility by default of being the oldest.

Recognizing that someone else is depending on you forces you to learn how to make the best decision that will accommodate all involved. Making these decisions is the first step to becoming not only successful but also independent. Those who master this technique early in life become the first to obtain the title of being so called successful. This practice over the years imparts the techniques necessary to make the right decisions through out life guiding you to the top or the top as you perceive it to be. But when you are subject to others and not permitted to follow the rules of your independence, you will ultimately look toward others to make your decisions for you. This may indeed be one reason a marriage fails or succeeds. A man without an example tends to give up easier and fall nearer to ill fate. Not recognizing how to fend for ones rights and rights of others, including his family. This may also be one reason that so many of our young men have grown to be classified as failures in life by falling prey to our prison system. Given that the definition of failure indicates divorce or constantly seeking the latest publications in the classified employment section. Not to say that one should not be a follower at sometime or another but one should always be prepared to avoid a collision should the vehicle ahead of them suddenly come to an abrupt halt?

07/1983—I consider myself to be a decent musician. I put all my efforts toward becoming the greatest. All my money went into obtaining the latest technology in musical instruments. Over the years my fetish had accumulated an entire recording studio located in beautiful

Denver Colorado strategically placed, in the living room of my very charming wife #2. As love would have it, on this particular occasion, a minor dilemma unraveled itself. Over time my wife's home had been transformed into the hottest recording studio in town. With friends coming over at all hours of the day and night and absolutely zero privacy, my wife made a perplexed disclosure. "Get this s—t out of my living room by the time I get home from work". I've always been one to oblige any request made in such a fashion as to cause the hair on the back of my neck to stand on end. Having the day off and plenty of time to respond I began the task of disconnecting and packing all my equipment into my old station wagon. As I mentioned earlier about not having an example in my life as to how to stick it out, this technique was the best way I knew to make the most out of my marriage. She came home to find me in the final stage of compliance. I'll never forget the joy in her eyes as the final speaker was removed and the imprints in her carpet revealed the true beauty of her demand.

But her request had been supplemented by the removal of everything else I owned prior to our marriage including my clothes. It all fit, in one load. From top to bottom, my station wagon was a rolling Carnegie Hall and that is when I performed my finale. "Where my equipment goes, I go" I said as I took one final look at my reflection in the bathroom mirror. This was a bit much for her to handle. The news of my announcement exit stage right caused a mussel spasm to develop in her right fist directed toward the left side of my face. Her display of subconscious love for me made it difficult for me to maneuver a swan dive over the toilet and scaling the tub in an effort to evade the issue at hand, that is, until I could maneuver passed her, but not without her finally confiscating my left sleeve to remember me by. My old station wagon didn't look the best but it served as an excellent get away car. Making a pit stop at a near by ambulance station, they bandaged my arm and asked if it were necessary to contact animal control. For those of you inquisitive enough to ask me as to the final conclusion of the event should you see me at a book signing? We were divorced shortly after and I ruined a beautiful relationship with a, at the time, three year old daughter. This separation accumulated a child support debt of over twenty-five thousand dollars due to principle and interest charges. To be continued . . .

Right about now, you may be asking yourself, what does all this have to do with getting out of debt? Well, the whole premise of this process indicates that by living in your car, you are saving the money that you would have been spending on rent or mortgage. Sounds simple doesn't it? Anybody who does not pay housing could save the money and apply it to the bills accumulated and therefore, free ones self from debt.

However, deciding to get out of debt by living in your car is somewhat like leaving home for the first time. The whole world seems different, bigger, more complicated once you're out there on your own. I hear people say all the time that life goes by so quickly but, when you are in your car day and night, time passes so very slowly. At times it even comes to a dead halt.

As mentioned previously, it involves a plan and the key to a successful plan is to stick to it so, I have also included with this plan a database with the process I used to complete this program.

Your situation will no doubt be different. You may have more or less time to spend in your car depending on the total debt you are in.

I have been living in my car for a while but, it's taken me this long to finally get the psychology of the process to the point of actually working.

Now I am seeing that the program only needs time. Time to digest the negative balances occurred. This will happen automatically as long as I follow through with only one method. Continue to deposit into my automatic payment account the weekly amount equal to the payment requirements. I am giving you the program that I created to do just that. At the time of this writing, I am not completely out of debt. I am currently two years away.

I am also allowing you to view my actual obligations so that you can see what happened previously to my being debt free. The only thing I am not enclosing is the many drafts of programs that lead me to the final working process. All you need do is save the program to your computer and replace my debtors and figures with yours.

One question you may be asking has been asked of me before. If you live in your car, how do you maintain decent hygiene? How do you change clothes? Sleep, eat, and drink in your car without people mistaking your open window for a 'help keep America clean trash shoot' or some mistakenly backing up to your car to drop off there recycle goods? That is the magic of this book. If you were to meet me for the first time and did not know my condition you would never know that I was homeless.

For whatever reason, on the few occasions that I did divulge this secret, the person would suddenly gasp and ask that I repeat what I just said. In their mind I must have suddenly transformed into some hobo figure pushing a cart ready to kill for an empty aluminum can or plastic bottle. I have lost more girl friends that way. They tend to visualize you with two Michael Jackson gloves over a trashcan fire to keep warm.

Now, that I think on it. Maybe this plan wouldn't work for you. Maybe I'm the only one in the world who happened to make these decisions and the cards just happened to fall in my favor. I don't think so. You see, about two weeks ago a strange man approached me while I was preparing to sleep before work.

I think it is appropriate at this time for me to inform you that I am a fifty-year-old African American male. The reason I mention this is because I truly believe that some of the situations I am going to mention a little later happened to me because of my race.

Now, back to the strange man. The guy who approached me was white and the words spoken between us seemed to camouflage any difference of race. I was parked in the parking lot of the Burbank Library. He very cautiously came from behind.

After a while you develop a sixth sense when someone is nearing your car, so much so that if this awareness could somehow be contained and connected to a car alarm system, the inventor could become very wealthy.

CHAPTER 2

DRIVING RULES

RULE #1—LOCATION

The location you select as a parking spot should be in a part of the city where crime is minimal or at least not so apparent. Notice you did not hear me say I parked my car in South Central L.A. Why yes, its true a person can be hurt or even killed anywhere at any time for any reason. But why lower the odds by placing yourself subject to crazies who prey on the so-called weak, and believe me when you are living in your car, no matter what your condition, you are perceived as weak.

In ninety-nine point nine percent of the cases that I allowed someone to know that I was homeless, I was actually in a better position than them. More on that later, gotta tell you about the white guy. I'll say his name was Robert. Although, I don't recall ever seeing him before he said that he had seen me several times. You getting the feeling some stranger has been studying my sleeping habits.

Not only did he know my times of arrival and departure, he knew what days I would and would not be using this particular location as my sleeping quarters. Which leads me to another rule.

8

RULE #2—Stagger your habits

Modify the times and locations you use for parking. We human beings are creatures of habit. It's easy to fall into a comfort zone and let your guard down. After all, where you park is your home. How often have you gone home at the same time using the same route each day without considering the fact that someone may be monitoring your routine. And think about this, you've heard about some people in the same circumstances that are kidnapped or murdered and they have a locked front door and a roof over their heads concealed from the elements. You, on the other hand are like a beach whale trying to hide in the sand.

Robert, introduced himself and told me something that enlightened the whole perspective of my situation. Three words that sparked my desire to stay strong in slaying the shopping cart syndrome. Three words that encouraged to fight any thoughts of displacement. He said, "you are not alone".

If you can imagine, living out a portion of your life so focused on accomplishing a single goal, and someone you have never spoken to be able to totally empathize with you.

He told me about myself, not as a prophet or a psychic hot line member but as an equal.

Robert was homeless and living in his car. What was so obvious about me that lead him to this conclusion? I have never spent the entire night at this location. The parking lot signs in the library clearly state 'NO

PARKING BETWEEN THE HOURS OF 11PM AND 6AM. In fact, I have never stayed in this parking lot after 9:30pm. Reason being that my graveyard security job starts at 10:00pm. Robert said he knew by the look of my car. The look of my car! I always keep my car washed, its my house, doesn't everybody take care of their house?

RULE #3—Take care of your house

Your car is priority. If something happens like a break down, fire or theft, it's like happening to your house. Pay the money to keep your car running and driving to the utter most dependability. The last thing you want is to have to leave your house on the freeway with all your personal possessions in it where everyone may sneak a peek at your privates. And some even deem to get what you got.

Robert stated that he had been living in this parking lot for the past two years. He had a job, working at Disney. He some how missed an important aspect about me.

Although, I was still trying to digest the fact that I was communicating with this guy who seemed to know my dismantlement, I was also somewhat curious about how he was surviving in relationship to me. How our similar or different situations had gotten us here.

Wait till you hear this. He had left his wife two years ago, so did I. His wife was a schoolteacher, so was mine. He had a good paying job with Disney, full benefits, paid vacation and medical, I work fulltime for the City of L.A. with the same benefits. The list goes on and on. He even offered to hire me at Disney if I needed a job. That's where he missed it. Allow me to stick a pin in the peg at this point. I gots three jobs, mon. How many jobs you got?

Whenever anyone inquired about my job I always answer in regards to my security guard job. I never go into detail as to everything I do and I guess in reality I am somewhat embarrassed to admit that I work for the city yet I am living in my car.

RULE #4—Be nice but be private

It's always best to keep your mouth shut. Don't volunteer information regarding your initial situation. If not for anything else remember, you do not intend to be in this situation forever. Being human we develop a strong desire to make people feel sorry for us.

It is our nature to want someone to be concerned. The only concern you should have is focusing on your goal. Concentrate on getting out of the shopping cart and into the check stand.

At one point, I wondered if Robert had gotten past my mental force field one night and overheard me talking in my sleep. But no, he was genuine. It was just fate that those few words of support were uttered when I needed them most, or was it?

The Bible clearly states that you should be kind to everybody because you never know when you may be entertaining angels unaware. (Scripture and verse unknown) for you see, I have never seen Robert again, that encounter was the first and last although, I'm at the same spot now and then. My encounter with Robert also shed light on something regarding another tidbit of reality. There is a new generation of homeless persons out there. As Robert so delicately put it, the middle class homeless. Yes, our economy has opened a back door to people who have a sincere desire to live a decent normal life, but have fallen victim to the easel that frames a darker picture displaying a beauty only in the eyes of the beholder. There are people who are wealthy; with the ability to purchase anything their heart desires yet lack the very thing you automatically obtain while being forced to experience the elements of solitude. Peace of mind.

CHAPTER 3

HOMELESS AND THE LAW

White lights set off my bionic alarm. Silhouettes approach from behind. "Good evening sir, what's going on here"? Those words stand out in my mind.

A consensual encounter is what it's called. The definition of the first contact a police officer uses during an initial investigation of a suspicious circumstance.

The Burbank Police officer relieves me of my solitude and his partner in the gun down ready position just out of passenger seat view. "Ah, nothing at all just sleeping" Is my reply as my adrenalin begins to flow ever so swiftly through my veins?

The local police department may very well contact you. After all, you're in their territory and they have the right to investigate any unusual or suspicious conditions. Know that once they look inside it's quite obvious to them what your condition is but they have to make contact and what they see in plain view is legal to confiscate. Also, know they don't want you in their precinct. You're a bad influence. You bring down property value, litter up the sidewalks and you are an eyesore to new comers seeking a fortress to purchase. After verifying my identification they ask the age-old question stimulated from my drivers license.

"Are you currently living at this address"? You can't help but hear your subconscious reply "dah" yes sir it's just that I've got my apartment in my trunk and I'm on vacation. "Hey jerk, yes of course the address on my license is current, I just wanted to save electricity and water so I'm sleeping in my car to conserve energy.

I just picked this spot because it's the best position to read a book by moonlight'. I was caught unexpectedly, with out warning. What if they weren't cops? Allow me to interrupt myself for another rule.

RULE #5—In the position right?

As you position yourself comfortably in your seat. **Adjust the mirrors of your car so you can observe any actions behind you without moving your body**. This includes when you are lying down in the front seat. Position the rear view mirror so you can see if someone were to approach you from the passenger side. I find that most of my approaches come from the passenger side. Maybe because this is the seat they will want to sit in if you are carjacked and they want you to drive.

You would be amazed at what you can witness when people park close to you not realizing that someone is in the immediate area. One time two lovers pulled up right next to me. They looked around, got out of the car. She laid herself over the trunk, he pulled down his paints and they went at it.

When the weather is just right your windows slightly fog due to your breathing condensation. While this may make you feel more secluded, in reality you're a dead giveaway to anyone with brains enough to want to harm you, they know there is someone in the car.

I'm quite sure that these fantasy friends felt some since of suspense in knowing that someone might catch them enhancing their passion under the moonlight. What makes me think this true is the fact that just in line of my viewpoint, the girl and I made eye contact. That's when she really got it on. I don't think she ever told him why it was so good that night. They never came back to that spot again cause believe me, I waited.

Where was I? Oh yes, there are three forms of communication the police use to initiate contact.

The Consensual Encounter: The police officer asks you questions. Everything must be in the form of a question. He must even ask you if it's OK with you to pat you down or search your car. Above all, you must feel free to leave or not answer questions at all times. If he orders you, speaks to you in a harsh tone of voice, blocks you vehicle so you cannot exit or pulls a weapon on you it is no longer a consensual encounter.

A Detention: This must be based on reasonable suspicion. The officer has a particular reason for contacting you. As long as you aren't acting suspicious and don't look like the person or drive the same car as someone they are looking for, you should be all right. If the officer is simply asking questions that's a good thing. Some people get upset at the initial contact of a police officer and escalate the situation to the third form of contact. At this point you could also be eligible to win the silver bracelets, but as the officer may reply "These handcuffs come off as easily as they go on. This is for my protection and yours'. I always said in the back of my mind—if it's for both of our protection why don't you put some on, too.

An Arrest: This must be based on reasonable suspicion. If you win the silver bracelets, congratulations, you will soon have a roof over your head and you wouldn't have to watch your back except for in the shower. Let me also say to keep your cool even if the handcuffs go on.

I have seen situations where the cuffs come off after it has been established that you were telling the truth. But remember, thousands of payrolls are fulfilled because you give opportunity to be processed through the so-called judicial system.

We have all heard of false arrests where the person spends half their life in prison before they are found to be innocent. If you were an officer on a good payroll, what would you do if everyone you made contact with were a possible consumer and you were paid on commission?

My mirror technique works. Warned in plenty of time, I note a car pull up out side the driveway of the Burger King in Pasadena. I watch as the officer place a microphone to his mouth to broadcast my license plate to dispatch. I see the officers coming. The flash lights wave back and forth as they approach. I hear my name and old address confirmation in the portable police radio now getting louder. The flashlights briskly invade my quarters. Once again I hold back the desire to go yell "Boo". I know the routine now, I switch on the interior lights, and with my hands on the steering wheel I wait for that familiar sound of the consensual encounter.

"Roll down your window pleases sir". My attitude is as if they were late for their appointment, after all, they were, I been sleeping here for two weeks. "Good evening officer, how are you to night". These words silenced the flashlight in my face. "Fine, do you have some identification"?

RULE #6—You can't go free without I.D.

Always have identification. According to most state laws, if a person is contacted and does not have proper I.D. and mostly during the commission of a potential crime, the police have a legal right to escort you to their free motel until they can positively identify you.

Finally, a police officer that understands! All questioning dissolved the moment I tell him my reason for sleeping in my car. I don't know if it was the tax lien garnishment or the child support payments that convinced him but he and his partner went merrily on their way. Just out of hearing range I was able to acknowledge a pat on the back to each other and congratulations was in order. The officer, who approached on my passenger side, did an excellent job of coverage, as this encounter was a training exercise for them, as to how to handle a walk up F.I. (Field Interrogation). I was an excellent candidate to be used as suspect and gladly would participate again if that's all that transpired.

Don't think that people don't see what you really are. Yes, they know. Cops know, friends know, dogs even know that you are sleeping in your car. Think about it, you know when you see something out of the ordinary. What I'm trying to say is don't try to pretend that things aren't bad just live where you are and keep trying to do better.

I must mention that on another occasion, with the law, in fact, it happened in the very spot at the above mention incident. They came from all sides. Cops everywhere, guns drawn, at least five police cars this time. The outcome was the same but I never went back to sleep at that spot again, this time it got to me. Why keep giving opportunity for a bad cop to make you a statistic? I later found out that the manager had called the cops and told them that there was a fight in the parking lot. With me being the only car on the lot, who would they make contact with? The manager had contacted me earlier that night and asked what I was doing. People with roofs over their head can sometimes be very unsympathetic. Once on the streets of Los Angeles a County Sheriff contacted me. This was slightly different, though this was a consensual encounter there was an in depth background investigation. A

28-29 was requested to police dispatch and performed to check for any possible arrests or outstanding warrants. I was cleared but another rule would be adequate at this time.

RULE #7—Public or Private property

Always park on private property: For whatever reason police don't seem to have as much control on a private lot over public property. Things are a little more lenient when you're off the street.

I haven't said a lot about how you benefit from all this financially from all this commotion up till now so lets take a listen. The money you spend on mortgage and rent is probably your best recourse for achieving your goal kind of like giving yourself a loan.

You may have heard of an organization called Consumer Credit Counseling. This organization was created to help people like you and me get out of debt by taking all your bills and paying a small percentage of the monthly payment. Most organizations that provide the same service take a monthly fee from your payment for themselves. They call it for mailing out your bills but come-on, who mails bills these days? It's all done electronically. You agree to give up your credit cards and not make any other obligations until your debt free. The only thing they can't cut down is the very thing that got you into this mess in the first place. Tax lines and child support incur interest and penalties.

So as soon as you're out of debt, you are back in debt paying off principles and interest.

Consumer Credit sends each of your creditors a letter advising them that you are now being monitored and promise to pay the debt in full. Only thing is, paying only a minimum payment, now it will take you three or four times longer to pay it off.

Most creditors don't like this idea but at least they get their money. DO IT YOURSELF! Write a letter to each creditor. Explain your situation and make it clear that you fully intend to pay them. What can they do except continue to call you and bug you about the payment. Now days if this bothers you, if you complain, they must stop calling. But you need to communicate so listen to what they have to say then continue with the program, the program that you lay down the rules. This is how much you get and this is when you get it. Then STICK TO IT. Keep your word or you are headed toward another consensual encounter. There is no magic to cutting your monthly payments down. Yes, you still get calls at work from creditors, yes, you take longer to pay but at least you have all control over the conditions with no monthly fees to pay somebody that gets money you could have used to pay off a bill.

CHAPTER 4

VOLUNTARY EVICTION

On the very first payday of your excursion, obtain a storage facility. Move everything in, keep only the necessities to survive in your car. You will need clothing to last you a week or so. You can go to your storage unit weekly to change supplies. Now you can afford a storage unit. You have put your rent in the bank. Go to the storage unit as often as you like to get what you need in order to let your car look like you are not homeless.

If you happen to go to your storage unit late at night and you're just too tired to drive back to your parking lot. Stay there and sleep in the comfort of a locked facility. 'What the heck are you saying Steve', that's right baby—most storage facilities are zoned for residential area. If you are paying rent in a storage unit you have the right to sleep there. 'Wait a minute Steve, if I can sleep in my storage unit, what was all that mumbo jumbo about the cops'? Well, if you get shot in your storage unit it may be that your body is not found until the first person comes to deliver a load. If you get shot in the parking lot of Rite Aid chances are that someone will hear it and get you medical attention right away. Let me stick a peg here!

I know this may sound a bit erroneous but believe it or not; there are a few advantages to having a change of clothes where ever you go. On one occasion I was simply speaking with someone who knew of an available means of obtaining enough cash to pay off one of my bills but, an interview was necessary NOW! Like superman in a phone booth, I simply parked in an alley and performed my quick-change artist act. In ten minutes I was looking like executive Joe. Had I had to go to a residence, no matter how close, I may not have gotten the job.

Obtain membership in a 24-hour health facility you can afford it now. This is how you stay fit and trim also a means of maintaining proper physical hygiene. Make sure the facility is actually open 24-hours 7 days a week. Otherwise, you may find yourself calling into work late as you wait for the place to open just so you can take a shower. Therefore, you are not running your fellow co-workers out of the building from over night perspiration.

With the rest of your rent or mortgage money take each creditor and pay a third through automatic distribution at your bank. If you owe $75 dollars pay $25 dollars despite the fact that they may only ask for $12 dollars. This is an easy assignment when you have automatic deposit, all you do is sit and wait for the payoffs to roll in.

At this point you should still have a small lump sum in your hot little hands. Take out for food then start with the smallest balance first. The practical and best way is to pay off the debt with the highest interest first but—you deserve to see positive results NOW! Pay the smallest first and feel a since of gratitude and pride that you have accomplished something for all your consensual encounters you've experienced this month. Pay whatever is left over toward that smallest balance first.

When that bill is paid off apply the additional monies to the next smallest bill and so forth. This sounds easier than it is but the name of this game here is patience and perseverance. One day you hold your yearning to piss until the gas station opens up. The next day you pay off a bill. Somehow, they are both a huge relief. Make sure you are checking with your creditors as to the payoff balance before you start applying extra money. You don't want to over or under pay a supposed pay off at this time. To over pay means you loose an opportunity to pay off another debt. To under pay means you may have added a late fee which will defeat your purpose.

Another payday comes and goes, so slowly time passes to reach my mark. What about when it's over. What happens when that last check mark is made on my payoff sheet? As one great man once said "I have a dream".

I have also created a list of equipment I will be purchasing to produce films. Right next to the spreadsheet used to pay off my debt, I have another one to get me back in debt, at least without further obligation. This system is improvised to pay off everything I will need over a period of one year. Lights, camera action another dream begins. I feel that the best way to accomplish this is to purchase rather than rent equipment for my movies. I figure, as many times as I would rent something I could have owned it out right.

I continue to educate myself regarding the art of filmmaking (spend a lot of time in the library. They are air conditioned in the summer and you will meet other homeless people there).

The original debt payoff plan is set for two years. The equipment payoff is set for one year. The total cost of equipment will be approximately $85,000. So now you know my yearly income between all three jobs. No! it's not easy but how long will I live? What if I get lucky and live another three years anyway. It would be a shame to abandon the debt relief plan and in three years still be in the same predicament, as I would have if I had not started the plan. What if this fiasco really works? Hard to say, life throws you so many curves. There are actually times when you're not all that excited to go to bat.

There will always be something coming along to keep you from achieving your goal. For instance, this may sound somewhat cruel to you but this is January, I have yet to buy my son a Christmas present. He's sixteen years old and up to now every year I would give him $100 dollars to do with as he pleases. I know that's not a lot of money but when you consider the monthly payment of his cell phone, snowboards, season passes, and extra $40 placed in his savings account each month it adds up to something I think lots of kids his age would give up their favorite Nintendo game for.

Please don't feel bad if you can't cram in three jobs as I am doing. It all depends on how badly you want out of debt and into your dream. And how strongly you feel that when you are out of debt you have a plan to achieve other goals. In a way the sad part about getting out of debt in the prescribed fashion is you know that you don't really get out of debt, you only make room for other debts. For instance, after I obtain the equipment for filmmaking, I'm going to have to purchase a house to keep it in.

About now some of you may be asking why don't I buy the house when I first achieve the debt free status? If you think about it, it would be very hard for me to obtain the equipment I need after I am stuck with a 30-year mortgage.

It's kind of like I've always thought about getting married. Two people dedicate their lives to each other spend a small fortune on the wedding then go into a mortgage or rental situation with outstanding debts. Not only from the wedding but also the debts they bring to each other individually. But I guess true love over comes the stress of bills due each month and heaven forbid a new baby on the way.

I figure most people knew each other prior to getting married which would mean not in so many words, WHAT THE HELL IS THE HURRY? You've already done everything you would do as if you were married except maybe purchase things in both names, which spells more debt! So why not sit down with a plan before you say "I do"? Pay off your individual debts together, this may even give you time to see something in each other you needed to know anyway. After being debt free now you know the two of you have what it takes to stick it out. Save up the money for the wedding. It really shouldn't take long now since you now have no other obligations accept maybe rent. If you are paying separate rents and you are not already living together I say one or both of you, move back with mom or share a friends place. I don't say do the car thing, even though that would definitely prove your love for each other. Mom and dad are sure to understand when they see how responsible you are and it's all on paper as to your plan.

May I add, have a set goal, and a definite time that you will be moving out. And if you are victim to one of us using this technique, for goodness sake, put it in writing (an agreement) a move out deadline for your guests.

I know of a story of two people who moved into a friend's house for a convenient amount of time. After several months they decided to stay. I mean stay! It got so bad that the owners moved out of their own house and stayed someplace else and pursued legal help to get the guest out.

Well guess what? The courts ruled that the guests now had legal right to live in their new home. It wasn't until after foreclosure that the previous owners had the house vacated and adopted a new FICA score.

After, saving enough money for the wedding its time to go shopping. Visualize together the floor plan for the house of your dream. Notice I said house; I feel that the purchase of property should be your ultimate goal.

Apartments are just going to continue to take away from what you've already been so diligent to achieve and after investigating rental payments, there is lots to be said about the monthly comparison between rental and mortgage payments. But, not so fast, how many times have you heard of the couple that moves in together then eats dinner on box crates. Old school says it's cute, romantic, everyone should experience it at least once. Hogwash, why wait for some financial miracle to occur in order to buy a bed or table? Why purchase piece by piece until everything in your house including your house is paid off. Hell, by then it's time to buy new furniture and start all over again. Together pick out the furniture you would like, everything from kitchen to garage. Jot down the prices and get into position to make the purchases all at one time. Now that's a good feeling.

But wait there's more! Now that you've saved the money for creature comforts you would have absolutely no problem inviting mom and dad, friends and neighbors over right away. No reason to explain how cute and romantic it is to eat on a crate box. Show the world you got it together even before you got married.

I jumped ahead a little. Yes, your furniture may be gone by the time you intend to buy it. But, I guarantee you one thing, the person who stole that perfect couch you searched so hard for, that person is going to make payments on it.

Remember, the perfect couch that you saw was not the one and only. Believe it or not, they are making beds, tables and chairs everyday somewhere. This experience will teach you how to compare prices amongst sales floors, so welcome to the world of managing debt.

CHAPTER 5

SUCCESS UNAWARES

Out of debt and money in the bank for comforts lets take it to the limit. Go house shopping. Little did you know that secretly hidden in the process you have just completed, you have raised your FICA score, this will definitely improve your chances for loan approval. It should be perfectly clear by now how much money you will have for a mortgage payment. Just look at your last savings statement deposit.

Whatever you are saving, add your rent and storage payments to it. Two thirds of that is what you can afford for a house payment.

Example: You are both debt free, you have thus far been able to save $1200 per month toward creature comforts, you have been paying $150 per month for storage since one or both of you have moved in with mom or a friend. You will have $1350 free to spend. But I said only two thirds should go toward mortgage payments. That's because with the purchase of any home you must include utilities, repair, and the unexpected. That leaves you with a $900 a month mortgage payment. Yes, that's impossible but hopefully your condition is far better than that. If not maybe the following information will allow you to increase your current income.

For those of you still reading maybe contemplating getting a refund or returning this book to the library. I thought you might be interest in seeing what my schedule actually entails:

I pay my bills weekly so I can see results that keep me interested in continuing this fiasco. I heard somebody say once that if the entire world were to shut down employment to just the bare necessities that only three careers would withstand the test to continue. Law Enforcement, medical and security positions would be the only careers to survive.

If you were so inclined to be able to enlist for an additional means of income to help deliver you from debt, you would have absolutely no problem working a security job opposite your regular work schedule. Now, my daily master plan, this list may not show driving time or time dedicated to personal hygiene.

I should also mention that I never at anytime had any problem with a representative from the health spa even knowing that I was sleeping in their parking lot. As long as my card went through every time I entered it was assumed that I was paying my bill on time and that's all that seemed to matter to them. Also, you will be amazed at how many people you will see coming in to take a shower without working out. You soon realize that as Robert put it so eloquently 'You are not alone'.

Below is my life schedule I just wanted you to see why I'm the way I am now. The sole purpose for the following schedule is for you to adapt the schedule to your specifications:

DAILY SCHEDULE

Monday
6:00am-4:30pm Video Production Job
5:00pm-12mid Sleep (Spa parking lot)
12:30am-5:00am Health Spa, shower

Tuesday
6:00 m-4:30pm Video Production Job
5:00pm-9:30pm Sleep (Spa parking lot)
10:00pm-5:00am Security Job
5:15am-5:45am Health Spa

Wednesday
6:00am-4:30pm Video Production Job
5:00pm-12mid Sleep (Spa parking lot)
12mid-5:00am Health Spa

Thursday
6:00am-4:30pm Video Production Job
5:00pm-9:30pm SLEEP (Spa parking lot)
10:00pm-5:00am Security Job

Friday
6:00am-4:30pm Library, movie etc.
4:30pm-9:30pm Sleep (Spa parking lot)
10:00pm-6:00am Security Job

SATURDAY
6:30am-7:30am Sleep (Spa parking lot)
8:00am-4:00pm Security Job
4:00pm-9:30pm-Sleep (Spa parking lot)
9:30pm-6:00am Security Job

SUNDAY
6:30am-7:30am Sleep (Spa parking lot)
8:00am-4:00pm Security Job
4:30pm-9:30pm Sleep
10:30pm-6:00am Security Job

Total income for the week $1200

So now you see why I originally stated that
this method of getting out of debt is very
limited to a specific clientele. If you decide
to take on this method utilizing your one
and only current job, let me give a word of
caution. Under no circumstances should you
start getting further in debt while working
this process.

It would be a disadvantage for you to bring
your debt up to your income. This in turn
would force you to continue to keep up such a
pace until you are out of debt again.

You should always consider the question, if
you were to lose your jobs today, could you
survive making a lower income. The answer should
always be yes. Just because you're making more
money than you ever have does not give you the
right to destroy your mental status by being
freed from one master and sold to another. The
entire purpose of gaining the extra income is
to expedite the elimination of debt. In some
way, that is my greatest fear, that after
living under these conditions for so long that
I may become accustomed to living in my car
even after I'm free. Like the reality of being
freed from slavery yet deciding to stay on

the plantation because I don't know anything else.

RULE #8—Take time to learn

Use this opportunity to educate yourself. You think I chose the library parking lot because of the shade? I once heard that if a person is on a job for more than a year without increasing his/her knowledge of the job you are not growing with the pace of technology. You are never going to be worth the position and may be jeopardizing your net worth on the job. Things are changing every day. New ways to perform the same operations are constantly popping up.

You can easily be replaced by someone with more know how. Use the lonely time to read on the subjects that you utilize on your job or in this case jobs.

Speaking of technology, today's means of entertainment have evolved into portability. Such that you can purchase (Oh no the P word) a small DVD player at a reasonable cost of say around $150. Most portable DVD players have a connection that can be used in your car's lighter socket. In our situation it would be an advantage to make such a purchase to help pass the time and maintain sanity. Most libraries have a DVD rack and for our benefit, they are free or at least no more than a couple of bucks to rent. Because of my desire to produce films, I watch a movie every other day. I like the director's commentaries; they help me to learn filmmaking. Books, books, books, I have never read so many books.

Next month I start school. Now you can call the men in white suits! Settle down, I'm not suggesting that you include school in your heavy schedule. As you can see according to my work report, I have two nights that I actually have to sleep in my car because of the graveyard security work. You want to keep busy. You want to do things that make money, keep you out of the car at night or increase your knowledge. So it's really not so bad when you consider living out of your car.

May I make another suggestion in seeking additional employment? If at all possible, at least attempt to find work at an eating establishment. This means that you can eat at a lower cost. Living out of your car of course means that you will be eating out each night. Please forgive me if my situation is so unique but I feel I must mention this aspect for my own ease of mind.

The headlines in today's paper were of some concern to me. The LAPD knocked down makeshift tents of the homeless. They arrested 50 people after telling them to leave from the down town area. These were of the lower class homeless, the untouchables as the police display their rubber gloves. I only say that not to degrade but to further mention that there is evidence of a new generation of homeless persons, called the middle class homeless as mentioned previously. The information reads that the reason for the disposition, according to LAPD; prostitution, drug traffic and burglaries has increased since this homeless camp evolved. Not to mention the eyesore for the acceptable to complain about during their scouting for new residential property. I have as yet to hear reports of our kind. I'm talking about those who have jobs, families to support and do not do drugs or prostitution. I'm sure the day will come but whenever I hear of homeless on the news or in print, they always refer to the cliché of the shopping cart syndrome.

No one seems to have an answer for the homeless yet even though they are deported from one section of the city they are still alive. So they must go somewhere, where? The thought crossed my minds that if these lower class homeless *(no disrespect intended)* are being evicted from existence what may happen to the middle class. Are we next? Is their misfortune a preview of what is to come? Will charters soon read, "Termination is proof of a life with no roof"? For the LAPD to do such a thing it must be the law that you cannot sleep on the sidewalk. Wait a minute, the people who were removed from the sidewalks because of the law must be the first of a major movement because, not two miles away in downtown L.A. there are hundreds of people allowed to do the same thing. Let me cut to the chase; those people who were cast out were in a prime residential property location. It is not the fact that you sleep on the sidewalk, it's how valuable the sidewalk can be that matters.

CHAPTER 6

WHAT IS PRIORITY?

Today the President announced the intention of dedicating one billion dollars toward the space program and the possibility of taking up residence on Mars. Behold the answer to the homeless problem. The first person to invent a bubble that fits over a shopping cart wins a free trip. Removing you from sight removes you from mind. How about that?

Here's a thought for us middle class untouchables, how about a parking garage. You pay $150 per month rent. You pull in to your numbered stall, which just fits your car. You close the door behind you for safety lockable from the inside yet will open with managers key in case of emergencies. You connect a hose to your exhaust pipe leading to the chimney above in case you need heat. Your dome light is your source of lighting, no need to worry about your battery dying; it's connected to an external source you just clip the terminals to your battery. You have just enough room to open your doors and walk around your car. The video camera pointed at your stall helps to prevent crime and protects the single lady who reads this book. One door out leads to a common hallway, which suffices as an emergency exit. What's that you say? Restroom? OK, lets extent the room to contain a Port-a-potty. By the way, that hose leading from your exhaust? Have the exhaust flow from your car to the upper portion of the Port-a-potty before exiting the building, this will cause a negative airflow keeping your new home smelling fresh and clean. OK, I'm awake now dream is over.

RULE #9—Make sure you have a place to go

Make sure you scout your parking dwelling place for restroom facilities. This is an easy fix. Almost any business must provide a public restroom facility for its patrons. You may have to plan your bathroom breaks. I visit the library as often as time allows at 5:00 pm. Even if I don't have to go, I go. I have been caught on a few occasions in very uncomfortable conditions forced to remain in such conditions until a business establishment opens for the day. The only real problem I have found is on a legal holiday, on a few occasions not following my own rule, I have indulged myself in utilizing man's most relieving slogan. "The world is our urinal".

CHAPTER 7

STAY COOL

This was one of those nights I had to play by all the rules. A white Lincoln pulls up next to me. Four Spanish gang bangers race the engine to show off in front of a couple of Spanish girls two spaces away, my car is in the middle. Tattoos and shaven heads cause me to assume the worst is possible of them. I breathe a little faster to cause more condensation on my windows for additional camouflage. A thump on my car is felt as I maneuver to see one of my drunken neighbors catch his balance against my car. They don't notice me, yet. They light up a pipe and the inside dims with smoke. I'm positioned in such a way that I can identify each one in court if I had to. I'm keeping a mental note of descriptions. You want to get use to doing this.

My observations would do me no good if I were not alive to relay the identities to police. I cannot tell you how many times I have had descriptions and license plates written on paper only to throw it away the next day because no incident occurred. For one hour I lay still watching, waiting, now I really got to go! I witness a little love play then the girls' drive off. An idea comes to my mind and their party is silenced as I raise my seat; get out of the car; and take a stretch pretending to just wake up. In full view I turn to see all eyes on me. I get back in, start my car and drive off. If I would have just driven off they may have assumed that I had been watching, spying on them. To get out and stretch would have seemed that I just woke up having missed all the preliminaries. Something else to add to your watch lists. The actions of these occupants could have certainly drawn the attention of the local police. Had a shoot out occurred my vehicle might have been used as a shield for both sides? Crossfire could have left me vulnerable and subject to a stray bullet. It would have taken me a little added effort to explain that I am not part of their mischief. In others words I would use the conditions of a situation to determine when it's the right time to do the stretch thing and skedaddle.

RULE #10—Witness to a crime

If you should happen to see the law being broken while in your car, **your only responsibility is to be a witness.** The above incident happened in a Pasadena parking lot, one of my bad spots. I can't go back there for a while. In this case nothing occurred but had something happened and I survived. I would have been able to give a good account of the actions of the occupants. I can't emphasize enough the fact that in many cases I was the only witness to see a crime take place. Of course, it's up to you to get involved or not but on a positive note, I did experience reporting to officers what I saw during the commission of a crime.

From that night on I truly believe or maybe I was dreaming, that on occasion I would get a flash from a bright light. I believe that it was those same officers sometimes checking to see that I was all right.

CHAPTER 8

BE PREPARED FOR ANYTHING

For whatever reason I'm awakened by a human head I see dashing back and forth in front of my car just beyond a brick wall. I'm unable to see the rest of the body due to the cinderblock barricade blocking my view. Now, fully awake I recognize that a man is looking into the window of an apartment on the ground floor. He stops for a moment looks into the apartment window then turns to look around in all directions.

He masturbates then continues his erratic movements. By now I have a description of most of him. I can't call the police, no cell phone. I make mental note of his description. The apartment light comes on and he scatters. A woman comes from inside and closes her curtains, his shadow enters her apartment. The light goes out. What a way to spend a honeymoon, the Newly Wed Game. I figure these two arranged this party as his entertainment, no telling how the party continued after she opened the door for him.

Rule #11—Have the right relationship

Throughout your endeavor, have a sure foundation in a relationship with Jesus Christ.

Another payday comes and goes, only 25 more weeks till out of debt land baby! I started a new script so I can begin shooting my film when I hit my mark.

This book is dedicated to all those who have lost there lives while sleeping in their car.

Today's headlines talks about how the LAPD took down several homeless sheds. Once again the homeless complain about being removed from shelter. Those standing their ground were arrested and given the cement roof downtown.

So, once again we are an eyesore to the pockets of the local communities we live in. I had heard about this shelter, located near the freeway at 8th street and Bixel, near the Staples Center Arena. Just so happens my part time security job was located on that corner. Notice I said my part time job was. I quit last week; I was working Saturdays and Sundays. A new manager took over the 600-unit facility. The new rules were to stand at the door and greet people as they would come and go. I lost my personal advantages to this job such as being able to read a book or study while on duty. I was transformed into the lobby ambassador. Here is my thinking. Yes I will miss the extra $4000 a year and yes this money represents an extension of time living in my car, I feel I'm working too hard at this not to have some sort of fringe benefits to ride along the way. I had also received a raise on my daytime gig which equals half of what the security job was giving. Yeap! Keeping the job and getting the raise would have definitely been an advantage but above all, don't you deserve some sort of gratification.

One important aspect of this entire situation is health. Nothing else is as important. Loose your health, you loose your job, you loose your job, you loose your debt relief plan. It's all for naught. We'll see how my body thanks me this weekend.

It will be the first time I leave my nighttime gig and get to sleep in, in the mornings. By the way, remember the work schedule I gave you a few chapters ago? To figure my current schedule, just knock off the job that indicates working from 8am to 4pm on Saturday and Sunday.

Rule #13—Have a purpose

If what you are doing is of no physical, spiritual or financial gain to you, it's not worth doing.

If I had not had my other two jobs to fall back on, I may have given second thought to quitting my weekend gig. Your conditions may be such that not having fringe benefits would not have mattered in this case.

On vacation from my daytime gig but not the nighttime gig. So for this week I am only working one full time gig doing security from 9pm to 6am. I am fortunate enough to have such pleasure. Off all day today was strange, my schedule fell in such a way that I got off this morning at 6am and do not have to work again until 9pm tomorrow night. So I retire early to my Pasadena parking lot. I get three hours sleep before I'm paid a visit by the close encounters aliens. It's the Pasadena Police Department. Showtime and the lights go on and I'm in the spotlight. Before he even gets out of the car I wave to him behind me and prepare to leave the area. He gets out, "You working this lot?" he says in a police voice.

So now what am I a prostitute? I asked myself. "No sir, I'm sleeping in my car". "Well we're having some problems with this lot". "Yes sir" I reply and turn on my lights indicating I'm out of here. At first I thought he was just using an excuse to relieve the community of another eyesore but indeed, on the way out, police were checking people everywhere.

So what was it this time that gave me away? There were quiet a few cars in the lot tonight. Aah I got it. It's cold outside just before he pulled up I remember subconsciously turning on my engine for heat. My exhaust was a dead give away. With me lying down, it probably looked like an abandoned vehicle with the engine running he just came to check it out. What about this other thing, am I working the lot. Not a bad idea, even if it was an accident. In big white letters SECURITY is written on the back of my windbreaker facing the outside window. This is one of the quickest encounters I've had with the aliens. He didn't question me nor did he check out my license. Why didn't I think of that! My security coat hung up to show SECURITY OFFICER was my ticket to peaceful sleep. From that day on you could see my security coats hung up at every window.

I relocated to the Studio City lot by the health spa. I may have mentioned this before in one rule or another. I'm a member of a Total Fitness Center.

I'm probably one of the more fit hobos in town. It's the only fitness center I know of that is truly open for 24 hours 7 days a week. In fact I'm writing this chapter in the parking lot just before bedtime. I would have added having a laptop as one of the requirements for living out of your car but unless you are writing a book don't defeat your purpose by making a computer purchase. The library computers should suffice.

CHAPTER 9

ENJOY BEING ALONE

Went to Disneyland today. My daytime job had a special one-day free pass. Good thing Mickey Mouse doesn't have to depend on me for his cheese. I spent exactly $20.00 for parking, food and gas for all day. You never realize how pricey amusement parks are until you don't have them in your budget. Sorry Mickey but you'll have to make up your quota with those out-of-towners who don't sleep in there car.

I wanted to take a moment to let you in on some unexpected information I received. I got a letter from one of my creditors of whom I owe $450. They are on my automatic payment schedule. I don't know if that has anything to do with it but they offered me a settlement. Now, a settlement is when someone you owe money to allows you to pay a certain percentage of the balance and call it quits. This is a good thing. They said if I would pay 60% of the total balance they would adjust my credit history to read paid in full and on time. (The saga continues—will Steve Sloan do it? Where in the hell is he supposed to get $270 from on this ridiculous drive me out of debt thingy?) Lets look at it for a moment. I currently pay this creditor $25 per week. This creditor happens to add principal and interest at a rate of 20% per month. According to my calculations this creditor is adding $90 a month to my total—meaning that at $25 per month it may only take me 10 years to pay off this debt at a grand total of roughly $2000. You better believe I'm going to come up with the $270 to pay off the debt. The only figure I'm sure of in this statement is the $270 pay off. I'll let you know how I get it because I don't know right now.

Also, received a letter from a credit card creditor. They say I should be proud of credit status and that they are sending a renewal card. I don't know who these people are I haven't used the card in a year. Balance showed $200 owed but it's the system that is taking care of the credit rating. All I do is make sure the gun stays loaded every week and it fires on its own (just make sure there is money deposited to cover the automatic deposits).

Well, it's been a couple of weeks since my last entry. The American Dream is just under one year away. I heard somewhere that the dream has changed focus.

The American dream use to be to own a home but now it's become to be free from debt. Did I mention my plans afterward? Movies have always been a form of excitement for me as with most others. I truly believe that the gift of movie production is my niche. I have created a plan somewhat like the plan to get out of debt, in an effort to obtain all the necessary equipment to produce my own films. Lights, cameras and transportation are on the list of wants in hopes that I will be able to freelance my skills for money to purchase a mobile home. It shall be a traveling editing suite to edit on the spot and produce DVDs. Script to DVD shall be my new motto. Replacing the current "If

Hollywood Won't Except You Then—Build Your Own Hollywood". I guess in essence, my one-year plan to get out of debt quickly turns into a two-year plan if you include the additional year necessary to obtain the equipment. So, along with writing this book I am also writing scripts. Movies, Television Shows and Plays are also on the back burner. I just feel that it would be a shame if I obtained the equipment and had nothing to shoot. Therefore I must be ready, ready to call action to a new beginning. I just wanted you to know when you go to the movies and see the opening credit read "A Steve Sloan Film". You will be one of the few people in the audience who know the true power of persistence.

Received a letter from the loan holder of one of my two car loans. Ford Motor advises me that the payment due this month is 0 no payment necessary at this time. I am now convinced that the aspect of sending my payments weekly is the cause for their response. Although I will most certainly disregard their request, I appreciate their concerns. The payments will continue to be sent via automatic electronic payment through my bank. Let me also inform you that my monthly payment on this vehicle is $395 per month. I am sending $125 per week automatically. I didn't want you to get the wrong impression thinking that just because you send your payments divided by four that you some how miraculously get ahead of the game. It doesn't happen that way. I also need to mention that if you are able to operate your payment for car or house in this fashion, write them a letter simply stating to put any additional amount of the payment, that is anything above the required payment amount you are sending toward your principal balance. This will give you a lower pay off balance in the end.

It's Saturday, so nice since I quit that weekend daytime gig. I spend my time now writing and educating myself in preparation for the use of the equipment I'm going to purchase.

The setback: I knew it was too good to be true. How could this have happened? I didn't check my account this week and there was no notice in the mail, after all, why warn me that I was about donate $140 to my banks worthy cause. Yep! $140 over drawn. If you were listening to me regarding automatic payments, WATCH OUT! Somehow upon changing my payments to several payees, I double paid 5 debts. On the good side I may owe them less but on the bad side several others did not get paid at all. I mistakenly sent money to the wrong debtors and shorted others. May I suggest you discontinue the auto payments and simply pay your bills manually? Keep your electronic payments; just cancel the recurring aspect of your account.

In order to fix the overdraft I had to call from the customer service phone at the bank and explain that I didn't know what I was doing, that I was out of my mind, I blacked out.

I have thus far canceled my reoccurring payments and will pay by manually clicking the payment to my debtors.

If you were so attentive as to follow my instructions mentioned earlier, then you may also be overdrawn. Don't neglect to contact the over draft department of the bank and explain that it's not your fault. The guy in the book made you do it. Put the blame on me.

If this in your first time over drawing your account they may have mercy on you and remove the overdraft charges, it's worth a try. Sorry for any inconvenience I may have caused you!

Set back to the setback. So, I got board. I used one of my credit cards; yes I broke my own rule. As I mentioned earlier I want to make a movie.

I went and bought some software that will give me the opportunity to record multi track recordings. For my computer to work in my car I also had to purchase an interface module. Total cost $400, which I call myself loaning to myself from an extra check coming in the last week of March. I figured when I get the money in March I would just pay off the card right! Wrong. After installing my software about one hour into recording, my piano keyboard fried and as you may very well know, once you open the package of software you are out of luck for any refunds. My software works fine and I can still use the musical interface it's just the piano keyboard went bad. I had a new keyboard on my list of items to buy but that budget will not take effect until May of 2005. My extra check will be $800, so at least I have $400 to spare right? Wrong!

I got my divorce papers today. The court did not file as 'We The People' said they would. My divorce was final February 19th 2004, not

December 31st 2003 as planed. So what's the problem you say, alimony? Nope!

Settled with her when we split up by buying her a new car. Child support Nope! Did not have any children with this wife. Let me guess Steve, you are going to tell us, It's Cheaper To keep Her, right? NOPE! She paid for the divorce at a total cost of about $350. So, why are you crying Steve? I just had my taxes done last week.

I filed single. For the first time in my entire life I was getting a $400 refund. By not having my divorce final by December 31st 2003, I was still married into 2004, which makes me married filing separate. Verdict—I now owe $1500 difference and I have only two months to come up with it. Ain't life grand, you have to laugh at these situations or you'll go crazy.

By the way, started school this week. Feels good to be in the system again. We talked earlier about education and how you need to stay in the loop. Don't forget to take classes that directly compliment the job you are doing. You may even get your job to pay for it.

P.S. my pastor welcomed me back to church two weeks ago, he asked me if I had found a place to live since the last time I talked to him. I told him no but I had a plan that did not include a place of residence at this time. He asked about girls in my life, I told him there were none.

Last Sunday the sermon was titled "Are You A Eunuch? I Don't Think So" I thought any moment he was going to mistakenly say my name instead of the bible examples he was giving.

Unexpected pleasures of extra income prove fatal. After having my taxes done my divorce gave some relief but I also owe $2000 federal and $1000 state taxes. My jobs did not take out enough.

I have about a month to come up with the money. Here's my plan. On (Pay day) I will begin sending IRS $50 a week. It should be interesting to see how IRS reacts to this. I foresee letters stating that I need to pay in full and stating that interest and penalties will accumulate if not done so. I don't have it, therefore, I would rather pay the penalties and interest to get away with making payments of $400 a month until paid off. We shall see.

In the past two months, according to plan, two bill have been totally paid off. One even sent me a letter of payment advising me that my credit report would soon reflect the same.

CHAPTER 10

BY THE WEEK OR BY THE MONTH

Paying weekly instead of monthly has definitely had its advantages. One, I maintain a constant visual inspection of my progress and two, I have eliminated the late charges which occurred at times when I just missed getting my payment in on the required date. My original debt relief goal completion of September 2005 had to be extended.

It seems I miscalculated when my buy back retirement balance of $25,000 would end. After checking with my retirement office the actual date of completion is December 2005. The reason this bothers me is not the fact that the relief time has been extended, it's the headlines that bothers me. That place I told you about in Pasadena where I spend one night a week. The headlines read a guy was car jacked, handcuffed and shot in the head. This happened close to the location I hang out at.

Like I mentioned earlier, it helps to have a relationship with God, these days you definitely need somebody you can trust to watch your back. Trouble seems to be all around. I can't think in the little 50 years that I've been alive if I have ever seen things this bad. Sure there are spirits of evil, a riot here, a murder there but, something is different. Things are escalating and crime seems to be no respecter of persons. Sleeping in my car just two days a week is bad enough. Heaven forbid any of you who do not have the nighttime job to keep you out of the streets for so often.

A new bridge to cross: Did I tell you about the dentist? My new bridge exceeds my insurance total by $400. Guess where that has to come from. All and all, the unexpected finances even though they have extended by goal completion date, have not cast me out of my car and into the seclusion of residence. Besides the unexpected negatives there are unexpected positives. Three weeks ago my job asked me if I wanted to work overtime. It fell within my availability so I took it. The 12 hours of lost rest transformed into an extra $450 thus, the ability to cross that bridge.

I have always heard that time moves so fast. Not when you're watching your budget every day. It's hard to believe that one day I'll be indicating a final payment to my pay off schedule. I have to tell those of you following this plan I really got hammered with taxes this year. I probably mentioned this but because of the extra jobs I owe $3000. I really thought because of the additional retirement and claiming zero that things would be better but! So the moral of the story is, have a savings plan so you can send what you owe to IRS each year. I sent in my return already, with out the requested payment of course. I also started sending $50 a week. We'll see if I get away with this or not.

Transmission went out. Ouch, I don't have $1600 I told the mechanic as my credit denial comes sliding out of his computer. So, I'm off to storage where my trusty Ford awaits me. It's not economical to drive but thank God for it. The moral of the story is, along with the extra money you put aside each week for taxes,

 also have a vehicle maintenance fund with a balance of at least $1500 just in case you don't have another car tucked away in your storage space. It's getting expensive to be homeless. I honestly don't know how my homeless colleagues are doing it. How do people survive? I'm having enough of a hard time fighting my way to be debt free. I see the scare-de-cats robbing banks and jewelry stores. Those are the ones who don't have time to follow such a plan as you and I. They want it the easy way, but there is a risk factor for them that you and I don't have to experience. At least we don't walk into trouble; trouble just seems to find us.

My taxing problem comes to the surface. I'm going to have to extend my vehicle hotel time in order to meet my goal. Still making monthly payments on the taxes I was unable to pay in full. Have received no letter as of yet saying it's ok to do so or not.

To hell with this book! Please forget everything I have said up till now. It would be better to live like most of the rest of the world. Broke, barely making it, check to check, on the verge of bankruptcy. I have had to re-adjust my thinking on my financial plan. I don't know what I was thinking, I'm sorry I wasted your time. Go back to the storekeeper and explain to them that you bought this book not having read this paragraph and that I said to get your money back. It doesn't work. If you are out there in your cars reading this book, run, run back to her/him, whomever you ran to be free from. Beg for forgiveness at least you will have a roof over your heads. All right, I admit. I'm a hobo; I guess that's all I'll ever be. Living from pavement to pavement. I should change the title of this book to "How to support every thing but yourself". So what if another bill was paid in full on yesterday. I'm tired; it's getting to be summer time. I stink in my car, sweating in the seat. Hell, every time I get in my car after work, I smell me! I'm everywhere. On my clothes, even after I take a shower and drive to work, I'm in the air, I'm everywhere.

One time it stunk so bad in my car after I woke up in the heat, I had to fart to make it smell better. I'm tired of stinking. I met this girl at church, she seem interested. I can't even ask her out. If I do, I will have to ask if we can use her car. Then there is that age-old question. "Where do you live?" What the hell would I say? How do I explain to the woman that on our first date, she was already in my bedroom?

Most of all I'm sorry to have wasted your time. Not to mention whatever the cost of this book. That's one thing I have to say that I respect about myself. I never intentionally try to pull anyone under water with me; it's always by accident. But you've got to admit, I didn't try to get your life savings or ask you to will me your house or stinky car. Instead, I just put you in harms way. Out with the cuckoos and freaks. Just think, because of me you got an introduction to your local police department and made new friends. I guess it all boils down to we all have to do the very best we can with the life we are given and hope that God's grace will guide our path to a somewhat successful life. So long all. Have a wonderful life!

Next day—Don't ask me I don't know. I don't know why this, get out of debt stuff is not working. It looked so good on paper. I have rearranged my payments to pay once a month instead of every week with the payments divided by four or how ever many weeks there are in the month. I'm not doing anything extra. In fact, just this weekend I checked to see how much it cost for the 60,000-maintenance check up on my 1988 Ford Explorer. The manufacturer wants $600, which includes tune up; rotate tires; transmission tune-up kit; lube job; change the platinum plugs. I did all that myself for $45.00. So what the hell is going on? My records now indicate that I am almost two weeks past due from my original schedule. I haven't even seen my son in two weeks in fear that he might ask me for some money.

My ex-wife called, she knows I have no problem giving her money. Until now, I just didn't answer my cell phone when I saw it was she. That was almost a month ago and I haven't heard from her since. I don't get a lot of mail anymore. In fact, I have rearranged my mail pick up to three times a week instead of five. I'm not late on any bill, when I look at my credit card statements I can't believe the amount of money they have received but I know that I sent it. What I mean is a bill that was to receive $20 or $30 per month is receiving

$60 to $90 per month. Yeah! I know, that's a good thing but the damn interest is taking away half of that. Only $10 to $20 is being applied to the principal.

Still haven't heard anything from IRS. Though it's only been two weeks since I submitted my taxes they are usually pretty good about telling you how much you owe them. I had mentioned that I am sending payments without their prior approval. I'm sure I will hear something soon. Would they dare to let me continue making my own payment arrangement until paid off? That would take almost a year. Anyway, about now, I'm ready for anything.

It's me again. Haven't made any entries lately. Not because there haven't been things to say it's just that. WHY! why say anything? I went back to my old ways. Forgetting about the budget and switch to the American way. Buy as you cry. I got some things for my computer like a tuner, extra memory, and stuff like that, the things that will make me more comfortable in my car. I might as well, looks like that's the place I'll die.

Got a call this morning from my old boss, remember him, the security guard job at the apartments. He asked me to come back on the weekends. I forgot now what the reason was I told you that I left in the first place. Anyway I said OK. I'll tell you why. Not that I liked the job in any way, it's just that ever since I left all hopes of getting out of debt were eliminated from my vocabulary. I reviewed my budget a little while ago and still say I will be out by December 200_. I don't want to tell you that I will be totally out. I will still have child support to pay for the next four years. My support is not that much it's only around $250 but the principle and interest not being able to pay for the past 10 years will haunt me for a while.

I was having a ball going to two sometimes three different churches on Sunday. From 6am to 6pm I was visiting churches. Maybe this weekend job is the devil trying to keep me from getting serious. Thank you anybody who has been praying for me.

Wait till you hear about Chiffon. Unable to pay tithes in church last weekend I volunteered my time at the church picnic. One whole day spent retrieving my old D.J. equipment from storage. I took two days off my daytime job to do the gig. Sorry! This has nothing to do with Chiffon I just wanted you to know that it always helps to be involved in a fellowship or non-profit organization to help keep your mind occupied while you're getting out of debt. If you can't give money to such organizations you may be able to give your time. A few hours a week volunteering does the soul good. There is something super naturally positive about planting good seed. Now!

So I wanted to burn two days of vacation time on my daytime job. Everything's approved and I'm out the door. I literally got in my car, filled up the tank and drove to San Diego. Not caring whether or not I got lost or found I found myself on the peer of Imperial Beach. Food and drink receipts accumulate in my pocket and I make my final stand overlooking the surf

patiently awaiting the next big wave. Then
BAM, it hit me! Out of the corner of my eye
she just appeared. Young, alone and somehow I
knew inside that it would be OK if I did one of
those romantic clichés movie introductions.
"You work out?" Not really, I broke the ice
by asking her if she liked the beach. She
said her girlfriend she was staying with would
not be home until 12 midnight. It was 9am. I
asked her if she would indulge me by being
my tour guide around the down town area. To
hell with this debt relief program! More food
and drink receipts pad my pockets and we're
at a motel. Now lets get something straight
right now. At no time did I have any intention
on having sex with this young lady. She was
the one who suggested the motel; I suggested
the rear of my Explorer. I told her she had
been riding in my bedroom all day and now she
wanted a motel. Actually I didn't mind, I
wondered what a bed would feel like anyway. We
showered (separately) and there I lay two feet
away from paradise. For whatever reason sex
just was not important especially after she
now confesses that she is gay and loves her
girlfriend very much. I respect that as if it
were another man.

I just enjoyed talking to a human being and
she was listening. She was from Dallas Texas,
age 26, came to California to finish school
majoring in psychology. Maybe that's how she
sat me up! Set up, wow, wait a minute. Suddenly
the clock starts ticking in my head. About a
hundred feet from the peer where we meet is
the Imperial Beach Sheriff station. Oh No! I'm
an avid fan of the T.V. show COPS. No wonder
she didn't want me to have sex, she's wired.

Any second now she was going to say OK $200 and I'm yours for the night. Then the door swings open and the white boys come in yelling, "let me see your hands, put em-up". I suddenly realize what a fool I was, I had spent $100 on her for food movies fun and damn good company. A set-up; how could I have been so stupid, I just wanted a friend. I had hidden my wallet at the foot of the bed so when she searched the room while I was asleep she wouldn't get all my money. I took the car keys off my ring in case she tried to steel my car. The bathtub didn't work so she and any cohorts would have a hell of a time putting my body in the tub to drain my blood. People get $10'000 a kidney these days. This was it, I wasn't gonna let this bitch and a bunch of hokey cops take me down. All I wanted was company and a little rest from three jobs. I take a deep breath and prepare to let it all out, tell her to take her microphone ass back to the street and let her cop friends buy her dessert. I turn to look her in the eyes and I don't see them. She's already asleep. There was so much comfort to her breathing pattern. I just watched her sleep, a perfect stranger in my bed. This young girl was someone's daughter. Is there such a thing as a stranger's responsibility? With food now dried on her mouth she was totally satisfied, probably afraid and somewhat confused. I now didn't believe a damn thing she told me. This girl was just as homeless as I was and was familiar with using the excuse of being gay and being faithful to her lover was a defense mechanism to attempt to keep men, not like myself, from inflicting additional pain to her life. And somehow, I think she knew she picked the right one to sleep with.

The next morning I took her to breakfast. She tried everything she could to hint to me that she wanted to come back to Los Angeles with me. I had to lay my cards on the table; my life is no life to be shared at this time, especially with someone who may be worse off than me. Sensing her attempts had failed she wanted to be dropped off at exactly the same place we met. The conflicts in her speech were just too much for me to bear, not much made sense of this woman's habitat. My heart hurts for her and thousands of other women like her. No place to go, very few people they can trust. I really didn't know how bad it was on the streets. I made sure she had my numbers, and a well deserved, hug ended my new friendship.

My only regret is that I didn't hold her in my arms that night, who knows, she may have needed it more than I did.

Did I mention I spent $400 on the generator to power my music equipment for the church picnic? There was already power at the location. At least I'll have a generator for my movie making. That's a good thing. One less item to buy for lighting my sets, I had intended on buying a generator but not until after I was out of debt. Maybe it was fate that caused me to splurge, maybe God was saying now is the time for power, I grant you permission to spend. That's it; God is trying to tell me something. Could it be a miracle is about to happen and release me from this havoc. Yes, that must be it.

Checks are bouncing. The $400 used to purchase the generator caused me to take a few steps backwards. Good thing T.V. dinners went on sale this week.

Paid off Target. I'll be rolling in dough. This is the plan man. Like pennies from heaven my goals are re-established. My enthusiasm is spiking. My will to succeed over powers any displeasure I might have on the negative aspects of any job I work.

My church attendance has dwindled some since I started back with my part-time security job on Saturdays and Sundays. I get off at the same time that church starts at 4pm.

Last week I had a dream about the pastor ministering on how we should pay more attention in church. When I woke up, he was looking at me.

Paid off one of my three Capital Mortgage credit cards. I started with the least balances and stacked my bills accordingly. Every Friday is payday from the part-time job ($100 a week) and I use the accumulation of this money to pay toward the bill on the top of the stack. When I started this project I believe I was somewhere around $98,000 in debt. On this date about 1 year and 9 months later I'm at about $52,000.

Something weird is happening maybe you can help me understand this. I received a letter from one of my credit card banks in which I currently owe about $200. The letter started out something like this. "CONGRATULATION'S MR. SLOAN our records show that you have qualified for an increase in buying power. Your maximum available credit has automatically been increased $500. Now you can rule the world with riches beyond compare. Congratulations again, we have enclosed several blank checks for your instant use in obtaining your financial goal."

On the negative side IRS has informed me that a $2000 tax lien was in store for me. I tried to talk to them for help but they say that since I have a compromise in effect that there is nothing they can do and the money is now due.

All I can do is continue to send them the $200 a month in good faith and hope they understand by my payment schedule that I'm doing the best I can.

I neglected to mention that $5000 of the $20,000 that I have applied to debt so far has been used to purchase some equipment that will be tax-deductible when I start the business. I did tell you about the business didn't I? The Steve Sloan Lab "Starring You" is the name of the company I want to start. All flavors of entertainment will be produced there. T.V. shows movies, recording studio and live audience productions. I also forgot to mention that my ex-wife (oldest son's mom) continues to ask for money. Her other two ex-husbands don't seem to be holding up their weight with child support. For whatever reason she is afraid to take them to court. She has three other boys as a single mother. She does have a full time job but I have never refused her an advance in child support. I simply readjust the payment schedule so she will have what I owe her. I think that part of the success of this goal will no doubt be to always consider people and not to become selfish. This may be a key factor that I haven't touched on before but somehow I feel that it's important to be fair and truthful while going through such an endeavor, while driving yourself out of debt.

I got relieved of duty from my weekday security job at the golf course, I think it's called fired. My weekend security job found out about it and asked me if I wanted to work full time for them. I worked 7 days a week for them for one week. I still work my day job full time. Man it sure was nice when they let me go from the golf course. I just can't imagine what the reason was. They told me that the contract had ended. So why did they have me train a guy from the same company to do my job. I just don't understand. Could it have been the fact that I had to shower on my post before going to the next job? Maybe the alarm clock alarmed them that I was waking up to do my hourly safety checks then going back to sleep. I just don't understand it.

I seem to be busy with my scripts, presenting short skits to my church. Standing ovation last week with "Town Called Motive". My brother found me after 15 years, he was there, too. In fact I put him to work as grip.

IRS has given me two weeks to come up with $1200 or loose my compromise. At this pace I will not meet my three-year goal of Driving Myself Out of Debt but somehow it's not that important anymore. I haven't slept in my car for two nights. One of the men at church made me keys to a small church office located in L.A. I come in and have all the resources I need to research my scripts, write and even play music. I'm sorry to have let you all down. I pray I have not lead to many of you into the streets and now leave you in the cold. Wish I could be there with you, to hold you and talk about dreams and future plans, now would be a good time. It's cold and raining outside, I miss hearing the raindrops on the roof my car, it just doesn't sound the same inside this building.

Back in my car—I'm down to my one daytime job and weekend security. They call me often with work but I decline. I'm tired. Will attempt to make due with my current income as it stands. Goal will not be attained as planed. This morning I got up enough money to buy a Jumbo Jack. Ex-wife called last week to give me her new phone number, she was blessed with her dream house. She deserves it, she's paid enough tithes and offerings in church to own her home. I did experience a breath of freedom when four; count 'em four credit cards reported increases in available money. I had to use them again, IRS threatened to cancel my agreement if I didn't come up with $1200, I charged the money and paid them off.

Starting to notice something on the streets. I was sleeping in Pasadena when gang bangers parked next to me to party. I moved to safe and secure Burbank only to have gang bangers park next to me to party.

Did I tell you my job ended at the golf course? I think maybe God saw how serious I was about filming there. I was about to start bringing in film equipment and film during my shift when no one was around. He didn't want me to get into trouble. I really would have made a beautiful film there. I had already finished the script 'Lakeside'.

This is a real challenge of faith. To survive on just the one job with the City. Time will tell. I'm finding that when you have a lot of debt like me, you just wait until you get the money and send it in thus saving yourself the phone fee on your cell phone? The only right way is to not owe them at all. It seems like when you're trying to get out of debt credit card companies know it and thrive off of your mistakes. My credit union, can you believe this, two weeks ago I bounced almost 15 checks now you know good and well they should have thrown me out with the bathwater but you know what they did, they sent me a credit application. The next time I bounce a check they can get a higher interest on my stupidity by giving me a loan and pay off the cost over time. Isn't that like a loan for the loan? I can't wait until November, remember, that's when my retirement is paid off.

IRS paid me? My first tax return ever. $600 in my name, so what if it all went to child support services, the fact of the matter is that it's over. As long as I keep my nose clean that will never happen to me again. Right now, three months before tax time and it is time for me to start saving for unexpected taxes. Don't let IRS surprise you, you be the one to surprise them with ready money from your saving account to cover taxes due. Even if you don't need it at the end of the year, celebrate your freedom.

CHAPTER 11

OVER PAY YOUR BILLS

Earlier in this book I mentioned one aspect of credit card debt that I once held in high esteem. Over pay your accounts, yes I said over pay. When you pay off your credit card bill continue paying $20 or $30 dollars a month on the account. This will take care of any annual fees and give you a negative balance. A negative balance is in the black as far as you are concerned but expect a letter shortly after 6 months of this practice. It will be congratulations on your credit limit being extended toward an even greater temptation. By the way, just like a credit card company raises your maximum on a whim. They can also take your whim away. The problem with this is that it can make your credit score go down.

Example: The credit card company says your maximum available balance is $600. If you owe them $200 your looking real good because you look like you don't really need the money. Your credit score is looking pretty too and you can buy that new car with AAA credit because you have not used more than 2/3 of your available recourses. But wait! There's more. So you don't use the card for purchases and continue to pay them described in your new book, you now owe $150 on the card, good for you. BUT while at the new car dealers they tell you that you don't qualify because your credit score is to low. WHAT! Wait a minute; you have a perfect credit score wuz up? Sorry

Charley—while you were driving to the car dealer, the credit card company got mad at you for not charging anything in the past six months and at-their-discretion, lowered your available to $200.

It now looks like you are living out of your car. You have charged over 75% of your available funds. In their eyes you are in trouble buddy. You are an innocent victim; don't you wish you hadn't brought your girlfriend to the dealer with you? But you'll show those credit card clowns. You can't wait to get home to the phone. Once you put on your seat belt you pick up the phone and call them to cancel your card. You show 'em buddy! You pay off the entire amount and close the account. After you end the call you can indulge in the sweet relief of victory. In the heat of anger you have released yourself from another debt. They are glad to get rid of you cause you are of no value to them and you got the last word.

Or did you, checked your credit score lately. Now you have a closed account. That is the worst thing you could have done. Now you have no credit score. The name of your book is 'Bicycling yourself out of Debt'. Never cancel your credit card, if the company cancels your card that's not as bad as if you do it.

Suck it up and unbuckle your seatbelt we'll start over again and in time your score will be victim to a new lesson.

Well I'm back from Vegas. I really can't say if it was the right thing to do or not. Is something right because you come away from it with a greater understanding or is something wrong because you didn't understand what you were getting into?

I went to Las Vegas to assist my ex-wife with a production project. It was not a big benefit to me financially but what I learned, I believe could only have happened under the circumstances. It was all work and no play, well we played a couple of times but from stage productions to music videos I was involved in it all for the first two weeks. Then at the beginning of the third week of my vacation I allowed business to mix with our past relationship and all hell broke loose. I left her house in a hurry without even finishing her project we had started. It was bad, like it use to be, like the reason we divorced in the first place. Anyway, that's how I have this whole week to talk to you.

As it sits right now all my bills are up to date. I don't owe anything for another two weeks and I have written out my plan of attack for my next paycheck. I bought a new addition to my living room, an inflatable mattress for the bed of the Explorer. Sure feels good,

haven't had any police contact since the last time I spoke to you but those two weeks in Vegas at my ex-wife's house may have lowered the odds. I find myself seriously looking into retirement in another state other than California. Las Vegas was very promising as far as real-estate affordability. My ex introduced me to a couple of on the side video production possibilities to bring in additional income. I wouldn't mind but I did get a taste of the heat generated in your car in Vegas and there is no way I could survive so, the additional income would be off set by the cost of an air-conditioned room to rent.

I don't think a week goes by without me thinking of the month of November. If I just hold out until the 27th I just want to see the 27th come to pass. In case you've forgotten, the 27th is the anniversary date of my retirement pay back. Almost $1000 extra a month will appear on the paycheck from the City. If all goes as planed this point will begin the count down out of debt starting with my smallest balance and working my way to the largest, which at this time is the car that my ex-wife is driving. The agreement at the time of divorce was to pay the car off and give her the owner papers. That particular car loan was one of those deals you should never sign up for unless you know for a fact that you can pay the car off in half the time or at least double up on the payments. You see, this was a loan of $21,000 pay off to be over a period of 7 years.

I will probably end up paying twice that sticking to the plan but if all goes right I will have the remaining 5 years paid off in 2. Why did I do it? Call it LOVE! I owe $14,000 on the explorer over 4 years with 2 years to go. Both payments are the same at around $400 each per month.

CHAPTER 12

SPIDERMAN TO THE RESCUE

You know you're truly homeless when you know other homeless people by their first names. Spiderman was his name as he approached my car as I read a book in the park. A straight up come on for change, I mean this guy was good. I noticed something about some people who ask you for money. They don't give a damn about your condition or situation. I have the honor of replying 'hey buddy look I'm homeless too. Just take a look at all that s—in the back of my car. That's all I have right now'. They usually take a look and say something to the effect of at least you have a roof then they hold out their hand. Spiderman is an unusual homeless man somewhat conventional. You see you would know him coming from a mile away. He is the only homeless person who pushes a shopping cart with a bicycle with it's own generator. That's right, he carries a Honda 3000 watt generator everywhere he goes. The reason is that he enjoys watching television. He says it can run for up to 20 hours straight. Spiderman is cool; you can find him around the Brookside Park area. He even invited me to look him up next month during the UCLA game. He says he can show me how to pick up an easy $400 a day. I'm not sure how he does that but it will be interesting to find out.

I missed it, the game is over. I had to work the CSU game in L.A. with the police department.

71

Did I mention I ordered some self-help tapes to set my life right. The radio commercial said they would help me to get rid of all anxiety. It cost me $30 to send them back, about what they were worth. If I had kept them it would have cost me $90 a month for 6 months. That is totally unacceptable. Just because you have a bad day does not constitute you getting in debt and helping someone else get out of debt using your money. Kind of like buying a book that promises that you can get out of debt by living in your car. Doesn't that sound ironic? Here you are trying to get out of debt so you send money to someone else so they can buy the very things that got you in debt in the first place or even crazier, so they can buy the very things you are dreaming one day you can have enough money to buy. Chalk it up to another lesson learned. Don't purchase anything in a time of desperation. It's cheaper to talk to a friend about your problems as long as that friend is a friend.

Just can't wait till Monday. That's when I make the call to make that magic appointment. I heard about it on the radio last week. "I didn't have any money for a house," said the lady from Compton. "I went through the program myself and now I'm owner of the apartment building with four tenants," said the announcer. But my skepticism was in third gear by now. Listening to all these people tell their testimonies about how easy it is to get into your own home. I waited to hear the punch line regarding how much the program cost. FREE! Said the announcer absolutely free. "If you just do what these people say, in time you will be a home owner". Just can't wait till Monday, that's when I make the call to Operation Hope. This is an organization that assists you in improving you FICA score and financial counseling. "Hello my name is Steven Sloan, I heard about your program on the radio and I would like to know how to get started". "Congratulations Mr. Sloan, you've already taken the first step to becoming a homeowner" said the man from Operation Hope. That following Saturday I arrived early for my second step, the seminar was to expose potential homebuyers to the ins and outs of home purchase. For those long three hours I felt like I was about to make a difference for myself. From beginning to end I was taken through the steps of what it would be like to actually purchase my first home.

The thought of relaxing in a living room without a steering wheel connected to it. After a short information sheet they ran a credit report and made an appointment for step three.

Three weeks later I arrived to their office again. Everyone is so kind, they totally understand how hard it is to accomplish such an obligation. It took me all of three weeks to gather the requested information, W2s; last two check stubs; sign permission for them to keep tabs of my promise not to use my credit cards and I was on my way to achieve goal number one. 'What do you mean I didn't pay them back". The credit report showed that a check-cashing place I had gotten myself involved with years ago, I didn't pay them back for a bounced check. What once was $200 is now $400 a collection agency is involved. I agree to contact them and take care of business. I figure the best way to do this is to wait till I have the money in the bank then make the call. It was estimated that if I were totally out of debt I would qualify for a house at $315,000. That's about a garage, maybe a two-car garage. Somewhat disappointed I agree and start a new financial venture to pay off the check place as they are #1 on the things to do list from my assigned credit person. Also on the list of first things to do, is to pay myself 10 percent of my gross income and put it into savings. Now that, I think I can do.

The precious phone call: My son called me tonight. He has his way of telling me he has a need. He got another job because it pays more than his last one. I asked him what happened to his old one and all the excuses came out especially the ones that expressed problems with everyone but himself. He started college three weeks ago and is borrowing books from friends because he can't afford them. Did you parents catch that last part? He gets a job that pays more, but can't afford his books. Yeah right! Now tell me if I handled this one right. I quickly told him that I am very proud of him and am here for him when ever he needs help. He is going to call me with the names of his books tomorrow. Yes I said names of his books he needs and I'll buy them for him, I might be a father but I'm not a stupid father.

I forgot to tell you the good news. I won the lottery, yeah! I bought two tickets last week. One of the tickets paid $2.00 so I bought two more tickets with it. I haven't taken them in yet. If this book continues, you'll know

I didn't win enough to buy the house with no steering wheel.

Consensual Encounter: Pasadena Police Department. It was about 7:30pm. I hadn't gotten to sleep yet. In fact I had just crawled in the back of the SUV when my most favorite bright light came on. I waited for the officer to get all of his lights on me before I rose up and acted asleep. I made sure he saw me rubbing my eyes and yawning so what else could I have been doing. "Good evening officer" as I slid out the side door. "Good evening sir, you living out of your car"? Yes sir I replied. "Do you have I.D. with you?" Yes sir. I turned to find that I was now locked out of my car. Does this sound familiar? I reached back inside to unlock the driver's door and removed my Driver's license from my bag. After radioing in and all was well he made out a FI or Field Interrogation Card and asked me to move my car. I told him I appreciated his understanding and he replied that it's not people like me that bother him, it's predators that he gives a hard time to. He even gave me the name of a place to contact for assistance, precious something or other.

Why not, the housing thing doesn't look too good all I've got to work with is $315,000 what the hell good is that? Besides, a new experience may add an interesting chapter in this book. I do intend on keeping my agreement with Operation Hope but I really do feel bad that there may be no hope for me. You seem to be the only one I can depend on right now so, read on.

P.S. I started teaching acting to students at my church last Friday. Always wanted to help people learn how acting can teach you to pretend to be happy. Gotta go now, tears coming on, starting to feel the need to flush my old eyeballs for a moment, see ya soon.

8:30pm—Got to get some rest. Got my notes studied for Friday's acting class. I guess I'll go to the gym; maybe there is a parking place by now. It was full when I approached earlier.

10:30pm—Turn this movie off fool, you gotta get some sleep, it's a work day tomorrow. For whatever reason, after working out, I couldn't fall asleep.

2:00am—What the hell is that? I was awakened by the sound of a woman screaming in pain. "Help me, help me" as I arose from a dead sleep of 3½ hours. My blood doesn't rush like it use to in these kinds of emergencies. By now I've learned to first be a witness then act only in a life or death situation. The woman is attempting to escape from a man behind the building. It looks like he is a taxicab driver and she was a passenger. What are they doing behind this building? Two other men approach. One confronts the cab driver and one consoles the woman. She is now on the phone to 911. Oh-o the police are coming, better get out of the back and move to the drivers seat. Still watching yet un-noticed, she continues to scream. All four of them are crazy,

never the less she looks like she is in good hands. Gotta move the car, police will be here any moment. Keeping all subjects in sight I relocate. On the way passed the woman I break my cover "Do you need any further assistance ma'am?" I say still unsure of what the hell is going on. "No" she says as she takes off down the street being chased by two guys in a car and a taxicab. A block away they meet up again this time with the police. They take her away and I can't go back to sleep, it's going to be an interesting day and I'm just as confused as you are.

Had a wonderful day with my son and his friend today. We went down to San Pedro to rent a boat and have lunch. The boat rental was closed all day. Saved me $40.

Feeling somewhat frustrated now knowing that even if I were totally out of debt I would only qualify for a house purchase of $315,000. I still want to follow the Operation Hope suggestion of how to clear my debt and obtain AAA credit but so what. One thing I haven't figured out yet. What about the part about that savings plan Operation Hope wants. They wanted $5000 to open up a bank account for the down payment. Did I tell you about that? It's called the matching grant program. However much you have in a savings account at a major bank of <u>their</u> choice they will match it to assist you with your down payment. Why would I want to start a savings account to save money up for a house I cannot buy? Yeah I know what you're thinking. "Yo dude, what about a town home or condo?" Didn't you read the Chapter that explained that I'm a musician, I make a lot of noise, you know, drums, amplifiers etc? I'm trying to learn to play the trumpet. If

I'm going to make a payment of anything over $1200 per month I better be able to make all the noise I want and have things the way I want them. Continuing with Operation Hope program can only help so, I will try to stay focused but I will ask that question when I fulfill my first obligation in December by paying off the Check Cashing Service, contacting Operation Hope and telling them that I have done so, in turn they will send two letters to a couple of places to remove derogatory information.

Had a guy call me from an organization that helps you remove derogatory information from your credit report. He asked me if I was ready to change my life and that he could help. For only $1500 he would get me AAA credit in about two years. I told him of the plan I was current involved with. He asked me how much they were charging me. When I told him "nothing" he quickly got confused and hung up.

Three months since my last entry. Ever since Katrina, not a single police contact. Is it by the grace of God and his understanding of what I am trying to accomplish or maybe something said in unison of every roll call around the world. That thousands of people are now sleeping in there cars. It's not as unusual as you may think. I hear it every night. A car pulls up but no door closes. There inside, just like me, inside wondering what tomorrow brings. Sometimes hold the pain of the pressure of urine built up. No place to release or lack of planning. Amazing how the human body adjusts, in a few moments the pain goes away. But that's not why I wanted to talk to you. I wanted to express my appreciation for hanging in there with me thus far. I just checked my bank account. An extra $500 appears. What! How soon we forget. Remember the retirement, the payment of $500 every two weeks taken out of my check to buy back past retirement over the last three years? Well, there it sits. But it's not like I can go crazy and buy candy bars with it. It's time to get even more serious. Operation Hope kicks in. The layout is to pay off a bill every paycheck.

CHAPTER 13

DON'T LET YOUR GUARD DOWN

A good feeling but, do not let your guard down. Anything can happen. Did I tell you about my son? He was in a car accident.

He is okay but his car was totaled. He called me; he rarely calls without needing something. But so what! You know what I mean? He says he can't afford a car payment and the insurance both. So I'm putting him on my insurance. It's going to cost me an extra $1600 per year. But so what! You know what I mean? That's only an extra 4 months living in my front seat hotel. You got a kid? If they go to school, work, and not on drugs, what else can you do but help? I love that guy and the weird part about it, he'll never know I'm doing all this crap so he can have a place to play, to call his own. I got other kids but I screwed up. I may never see them again. I didn't know how to be a man, I think I'm learning real fast. I found the secret. Can't tell ya yet! "Dad, it's so hard catching the bus". Those were the words he said to me this morning. I called Steven, (my son), to see how he was since the dentist last week. Don't ask me where he gets the strength. I was never that strong, car accident; teeth fixed and ready to crash again.

It's been three months since my last entry. I messed up and met someone. At her request, I promised not to mention her name. She made me forget about my budget. We did everything on the weekends. She made me not care about keeping my promise to myself about getting out of debt. The beaches overnight, the restaurants and carnivals sure were a nice distraction. Several calls from creditors begin to come in, for not making payments on time or not at all. I had to let something go, I chose her. I had to get my focus back. I should be caught up in a few paydays and back where I started but I will never forget her smile.

I don't see the results from the extra money after having paid off my retirement payback. I was off a couple of weeks. You know how when you take on a new job you may not get paid right away? There is this lag between when you started and your first paycheck.

That's what happened to me. When I was told that my last payment would be on the 27th of November I did not take into consideration that the effects of my pay off would not be until three weeks later. That's about where I am now. That payday will happen in 5 days. But my car payment and other things are now past due. I will not be able to keep my promise with the Operation Hope people. I will have to take things as they come. I miss her already.

Fun time yesterday! I took the written and oral interview for Senior Photographer; heavy competition from the employees already working in the Photo Unit. If selected, it will mean an extra $10,000 per year. I don't put anything past myself. I'm a fast learner and very creative 'right'.

Sometimes things don't pan out do they? It's holiday time, lots of people having fun together. I went over a friend's house for Thanksgiving, I saw two people in love, and it made me wish I had someone.

At Christmas time, my supervisor gave me a book on still photography. "Ya think he knows something about the test results?" The test results came out today. 91% ranked number 7 on the list. But so what! There is only one position open as Senior photographer and those other 6 people above me, they probably already work in the photography department. It's all about who you know. And I know Jesus.

Yesterday was payday; I open my check to find tangible results. An extra $400 in my account. It really did happen my retirement is paid in full. Gotta keep my head on straight, stay focused, don't blow it, don't get into a situation where you have to depend on that money and crush your dreams of debt relief. The last three years have honed you into living with what you have. Now that you have $800 dollars extra a month what are ya gonna do dude? The American way is to call it quits. Get an apartment, a roof over your head. Ya ding bat ya been sleeping in your car for the past three years don't you think you deserve a break. SHUT UP! Is what I told myself after conversing for a while? I told my hands to go to the bank and get the $400 out of my account. I told my feet to operate my mobile bed toward the direction of the Check-Into-Cash office. I plop the money down. They say "And how much would you like to borrow now that you loan is paid off? Mr. Sloan, Mr. Sloan, you've been with us for a year now" as the door slowly closes behind me. It feels good, damn good. Talk to ya in a couple of weeks. I now owe a total of $30,000 debt to my name.

P.S. Parked at Denny's the other night. Two cop car pull up one on each side of me. They look in to see me sleeping; they go into Denny's to eat. They come out, they leave, and life is getting better.

Three weeks since my last entry. Things leveling off, no more borrowing from the check place. Things are due on and around my payday. I'm able to scrounge up money to make the payments just days even hours before they are due. Haven't been in this position in a long time. I have a good feeling about this driving out of debt stuff.

Haven't heard from that Operation Hope place. You know, the place that is going to help get me out of debt. Although, my agreement really starts on the next payday in about a week just after New Years Day, I'm suppose to call this check cashing place in Pasadena and offer to pay off a three year debt of $400. This was Operation Hopes idea. I could pay off two credit cards with $400 but they insist. They don't know it but it's already done. Come to think of it, I owe it all to them. Something about having a delinquency with a check into cash place is the absolute worst thing to have on your record. The Operation Hope lady had told me that with that unpaid balance on my credit, the banks will not even give me a checking account. That made sense to me, what the heck, I got myself into this mess I might as well listen to someone else willing to try to get me out, so I paid it off.

Gotta go, working on scripts. Pastor asked me to put on a skit introducing each of his messages for the month of January. I got a nice group of dedicated students. We still meet on Friday nights at the church.

CHAPTER 14

FOR WHITE PEOPLE ONLY

Darnit! The City only hires the white people for the good jobs. They hired this guy from inside the very office the vacancy was required, for the Senior Photography position. They knew who they wanted but you know how it works for city positions. The testing process is just a formality. Enough of that, I got a little juice for ya. Something happened last night in my San Bernardino sleeping hangout.

The Denny's Restaurant is where I go now since I stopped hanging out at the Salvation Army, because there is too much drug dealing. The roaming Negroes kept knocking on my window thinking I needed drugs or sex, or both. Anyway back to Denny's. The taillights awaken me right next to my car. This car takes several tries to squeeze between me and another vehicle one stall down. Mind you now, there are about 13 parking spaces all in one line facing, and every one of them is empty. This fool chooses a spot between me and the only other car. This was my first indication that something was up and I figured that I was going to get a front row seat at a vehicular sex show. I start panting hard so to create a condensation camouflage. It's been raining so all my windows are covered with droplets, this made for the perfect screening room. This guy gets out of the drivers seat of a fairly new black Lincoln Continental. I swear, he looked like the average mug shot you see wanted for child molestation.

1/1/06 0235 hours—I wanted to get this date and time recorded just in case one of you coppers happen to be reading this book and recognize this incident where a child molester chooses this night to graduate to older prospects. He is a Spanish adult male about 5'8", 180 lbs. Not to say that all Spanish males with this description are usually on the nightly news but I'm not kidding, this man was up to no good. There was no one else in the car. He goes to the trunk and starts fumbling around with something. He takes off his shirt and puts on another one almost the same color and style then he goes back to the drivers seat. He goes from the trunk to each of the four doors on the car, I swear for the next 15 minutes this was all he did. I kind of wish I could get a birds eye view of what was in the trunk. Maybe I could have helped with the description of a body in the trunk. That action really didn't surprise me some people just do stupid things (like sleep in their car) but what really caught my attention was the fact that, well let me take a back seat to this story for a moment.

About 10 years ago I worked for a major department store. I was trained in the process of catching shoplifters. Funny part about how I got this job. I was in the process of repaying my debt for bouncing a check and became friends with the security manager. Did I tell you about that one? Anyway, I became so apt to catching people stealing that after a few years all I would have to do is keep my surveillance camera pointed in the main entrance and watch each person as they came into the store. It wouldn't be long before something would attract me to an individual entering, just something about them would ignite this feeling inside me.

Don't ask me what it was but at that point I would leave my observation booth and get on the same ground level with this individual and do my thing observing in close proximity. I got a 95% arrest score just off of whatever it was that I developed watching people who commit crime. Some of you officers know what I'm talking about. Well—back to my story. If I still have that whatever it is, lets call it since of criminal activity about to occur, that was in me back then.

Well, back to the Denney's episode, the moment this guy got out of his car compared to the feeling I got, I should have call the FBI, CIA, BMW whatever. All flags went up! I mean this guy was HOT. But according to the law I had nothing, absolutely nothing to go on. There was a point in my observation that I mentally started documenting his actions because I just knew I was going to end up in court, if I survived. I started describing this guy to myself, as the on coming lights would hit right on his face I could see his eyes so clearly, his large nose and facial tones, I even looked for scares. He would place something around his waist then look around. He never stopped looking around, never. Then he did it, my premonition is never wrong.

He reaches into the back seat and pulls out what I identify as a case for knives. It's carving time baby, but who is the victim? It didn't take me long to realize that the victim was me. One last wardrobe change into a white smock and cap. It was shift change for the cooks. This was probably the parking space the chef has been using for years. I went inside for an early breakfast. He was a very good cook.

Changed parking locations. At the Pasadena hangout in front of the Rite Aid, two men fighting and a woman screams for help. I drive my car to the parking space with the screams coming out but noticing an unfamiliar steering pattern with my car; this parking lot suddenly seems rough. Two men fighting, I go into the Rite Aid and ask the manager to call the police, (don't want to use my cell phone, keep the minutes down). One man has a tire iron, the other bleeding from the face, the woman hysteric. I identify myself as an employee of the police department. The fight stops. Knowing that the police are on their way I begin to question as to what happened. My intention was to hold the parties there until police arrived. One man, the one with the tire iron tosses it in the front seat of his truck, gets in and attempts to drive off. A bystander maneuvers his car in front of him to no avail and the suspect takes off. I signal the bystander to follow while I verify that the police are in route. The officers show up and as I am giving them the license plate of the get-away-car I over hear on their radio that the bystander has followed the man to his apartment and an L-Unit is on location (Most police departments like to operate patrol cars with two officers per car. An L-Unit is a police car with only one officer in it). My information is given to the officers and they ask if I would go with them to the apartment to give a positive I.D.

My self and the victim I.D. the guy and we separate with her gracious sigh of relief. I get to my car and hear a hearty Happy New Year from a stranger along with "by the way buddy, did you know you have a flat tire"? I thump, thump into a space on the downgrade. The parking lot is soaking wet from the first New Years Day rain in 50 years but the timing of my tire change occurred between clouds. I get the job done just in time before the next down pour; thank God for the brake in weather, go back to my regular bedtime parking space.

Gotta quit now, my battery on the computer says I have done enough writing for one night. Tomorrow is a workday and my year has only just begun.

Payday today, everything is paid on time. Had enough money left over to look at using automatic payment with B of A. breath of fresh air. Starting to meet some really nice women at church. Amazing how these girls seem to be popping up suddenly at the same time that things are financially leveling off. I explain what I'm trying to do financially like not spending money on them but they don't seem to mind me living in my car. One nice lady says "you will always be in debt so you might as well go ahead and get involved."

That flat tire I told you about may be an indication that I need new tires all around.

Went by Cosco to check out the cost of tires, $360 out the door. Radiator went out in the Chrysler in my storage unit, $150 will take care of that. I have decided to get the flat tire fixed and drive the Explorer until I get other signs of failure. Just seems to me that I'm on a roll and should do anything to extent this pleasure to the extreme. I just have to hope not to get another flat until next payday. I would love to see that payday come without being forced to buy anything. In fact, the plan to hold on to all monies until the amount in savings equals the amount needed to get out of debt would really feel good. The only problem is that by waiting and saving for a year means that I would loose a lot of money in interest but just knowing it's there would be such an inspiration.

When I looked at the $14,000 that was taken out in my savings plan over the last year but had to be used for bills it would have been nice to have taken that money and paid off most everything I could have. I'm going to go for the big pay off way of thinking. There is also another problem with this plan.

$14,000 would also put me in the race to purchase that equipment to make my movies. Got to maintain and stay focused. I now feel comfortable in reviewing the option of making all my monthly payments an automatic payment deduction. I have wanted to do this for a long time.

I need to mention something about that job interview I had a few weeks ago. I concluded one of my thought by indicating that I felt

that I was going to get the job on the pure
fact that I know Jesus. You need to recognize
that I also believe that God also prevents me
from making mistakes and that promotion may
have been something that I wanted, not him.

Will somebody please tell me what the hell
is going on! Why, that's all I want to know,
why, why, why is it that every time I take two
steps forward the economy demons from the past
figure that this is their cue to kick me one
step back. The bank for my car payment says
they have to extend my payments. Evidently all
the extensions on my car payment have caught
up with me. They are adding extra payments to
my account. I guess I can't complain, it's just
that by not keeping an accurate account of my
payments I'm jeopardizing my credit rating.
In three more days my second paycheck will
be showing pay without retirement deductions.
Supposedly an extra $400, the last paycheck
didn't even make a dent in advancing. I just
don't understand it. I didn't even buy anything.
What's going on?

I just came back from the Check-into-cash
place. I did the cardinal sin. I borrowed $255
and paid them $300. That's stupid but I have
scheduled bill payments to be automatically
paid through B of A and I do not have the money
to cover it. My bills are scheduled according
to the proper due date and if that amount is
not allowed to fly at that particular time it
is an indication that something will backfire
on me like bounce fees. I use this method to
keep my credit cards current.

If you still don't understand, I simply schedule an automatic payment to occur of the date of the requested bill. The date to deduct the money from my account sends the payment off just in time before the due date. In other words, if I have the money in my account at the time of the scheduled deduction my bill will always be on time and enough allotted to pay the bill down considerably. Let's see what happens next week.

Payday yesterday, paid all bills on time with $200 left in the bank to last me for two weeks. Gotta give that money to a friend. She went with me to Las Vegas to pick up the car I gave my ex-wife. She calls (the ex-wife) to tell me that the car hasn't been working for a while and it's too expensive for her to fix. It needs about $1200 work. I spent $200 on gas to drive my car there and back and on the rental truck. Scheduled to pay $175 to a credit card next payday for rental on the towing equipment. My storage unit is going to charge me an extra $100 to store the broken van I brought from Las Vegas. Is there any consolation to life's madness? Damn that van is nice and big! I could set up a refrigerator and flat screen T.V. This is a Chrysler Town and Country that seats 7 not including room for luggage. My Ford Explorer loaded and designed with my life style leaves me with no room for a passenger. I spent $15 on software I found on the Internet. It trouble shoots you're car problems. Guess what I'm gonna try to do it for less, that's right I'm gonna fix it myself? See ya next payday.

CHAPTER 15

GET USE TO BAD DECISIONS

Bad decision spent the night over my friend's apartment accepting an opportunity to evade the cold. 4:00am checked to see if a parking space was available yet. There were no parking spaces when I came in. I swear, not a single space in the whole apartment complex. I had to park in the handicapped space. I figured that I would come out after all the party people next door left and there would be a parking place open. TO LATE! My house is now missing in action. I called the tow company to tell them I was on my way to pick up my car and to find out the financial destruction I've caused to my financial plan. $356 dollars, that's what a fool can throw away if you let him. Picked up the car and instantly began thinking about how bad it could have been. The car could have been stolen then I would have no car because after the insurance company paid it off there would be nothing left to purchase another. The thief could have totaled it and then I would have had to pay for the damage. On top of that, this lady friend of mine insisted on paying half of the bill because it happened while I was visiting her. So, life is good. I really do intend on paying her back. I tried to fulfill this obligation this payday but things just didn't come together. If it had not been for my car insurance payment due, $307 dollars, I would have had that extra cash to pay her. As of today, I owe that check-into-cash place only $100 dollars.

Got a part-time gig initiated from my friend. Gonna get paid for my hobby. This lady friend I just mentioned, she wants to manage my acting career. It's been two weeks now and she got me lined up to do some skits. One of them in two weeks pays $300. If I'm good, it could be a monthly gig. I seem to be mentioning her more regularly, I wonder why.

Remember the photographer position with the city. We'll I was wrong about them only hiring white people and the fact that they know who they want even before interviews. I got a letter last week; they asked if I would like another interview. To this date they have not held the oral interviews for the position. I mention this job because I am at my top step in pay in my current position and the only way to advance is to get a promotion into a different field. I can't afford school right now so I continue to look for advanced job positions within my present job experience.

This lady friend of mine, she admires how I am handling my financial situation. She catches me on the floor with my bills scattered around preparing to pay stuff. She asks me how it works. She says the thing that perturbs her is having to write the bills out and mail them. The next day I spend a couple of hours with her helping her set up an account with B of A and an automatic payment plan. We go to lunch and there is a sparkle in her eye. I think she's relieved that she'll never have to write another check.

I have added a new debt, the storage facility for the car I brought back from Las Vegas. It's

$115 dollars a month. You remember the one, my ex-wife said to come get and that will solidify the conclusion of any communication in our relationship, which by the way, was legally finalized about six weeks ago. She called me last night. Nice as a cuddle bug, said she just wanted to hear my voice. BULL-TWINKEY! I got off the phone before she could ask me about the car. My guess is that she wanted to know if I fixed it or not. All that sweet talk about how she catches the bus to work for a two-hour ride. I should end this book now and send it to her, teach her how to think like me. Things could be worse, you could be walking to work. You could be car-pooling with a fellow teacher and get car jacked and kid napped to another state and have to pay plane or bus fare. I still think I can fix the car but when I do it will be in my budget, and on my own time—case closed.

One month since my last entry. 'What in the hell were they doing in the recording studio when they recorded this song? It sounds like the musicians are yelling at each other'. It wasn't the music in my headphones; the screaming was coming from outside my headphones. I remove them from my ears only to hear that familiar sound of fighting. I turn to see a man on the ground being kicked to death by another man. Here we go again, this is a hot spot for crime at the Rite Aid in Pasadena. The kicker hops into his car and speeds off. He passes right by me. I'm close behind with no lights. I just need to get a closer look at his license plate. One block, two blocks, closer, I've got to get closer. No telling how the guy on the ground is but I see a witness on his cell phone calling the police. Paramedics should be there by the time I get back, if I get back alive. The driver now knows I'm chasing him. I look for guns pointed outside the window and a sudden stop that may give him an opportunity to fire at me. He runs a stop sign but not before I get the plate number. First memorized then committed to a piece of gum paper. I return to the scene of the crime.

The guy I thought was calling the police was really only telling his friends about all the excitement. The guy who was being kicked was gone. The suspect returns to the scene of the crime. The guy who was getting kicked to death hops into the suspect vehicle. His friend who just happens to be the guy he was kicking the crap out of. They move on to their next performance for another round of applause by deceived witnesses.

I put my headphones back on; chew the gum with a plate number on it and submit a prayer and a grin, 'Father—how much longer do I have to live like this'.

Three weeks since my last entry. My boss at the office says to check the messages as soon as I get in each morning. "I deleted some messages that may be embarrassing to you if someone else heard them." I look at the message he copied down for me from Ford Credit and Long Beach Acceptance. They both say the same thing, 30 days past due. Even though because of the way I pay them (splitting the payments so each one gets something every two weeks) it doesn't seem to matter. I call the Ford Company first to explain that I will send the balance of last month's payment next week on payday. They seem to understand what I'm trying to do but still say to wait until I have the full monthly payment and pay it at one time. That doesn't make sense to me, it seems that the quicker I get some money to the loan agency the better chance I have of hitting the monthly balance before a thirty day late fee is reported. They say they can extend my contract and bring me up to date. I've done that about three times on both car loans. I'm not doing that anymore. I'll give them what I have and accept the deal as the cards fall.

I called my old boss last week, the manager of the security place. I told him I needed some money to fix my car and if I was in good standing with his company? He said always! I told him my days off, he says call him Monday for my work schedule.

By the way, that gig that paid the three hundred dollars, the acting job. It went really great. The cast and crew loved it, the sets were beautiful and all three hundred youths gave a standing ovation. I paid each one of my students $25 for gas and explained that the difference between a armature actor and a professional is the fact that the professional gets paid something. They graduated last night, perfect timing. A stroke of luck how the class ended just before I am to start working another job. I going to bounce back, one day, I'm busting out of this hole.

Tomorrow is payday; I have programmed my B of A account to take care of everything except the two car payments. I'm going to have to think about this a little more. Haven't gotten a concrete schedule from Jim my security job manager about working more hours. Got my appointment for the Senior Photographer position, it's next Thursday.

Tomorrow is the day, I took off work today to spend as much time as possible studying how to be a leader and photograph crime scenes and stuff like that to be sure to pass my interview. Found out yesterday that my current boss in the video unit is going to be on the oral panel for my photographer test tomorrow. Is that good or bad? I just realized that this book I'm writing is turning into my damn diary. Let's see, stay focused, finances.

CHAPTER 16

A DAY OF FREEDOM

This month marks the free paycheck. No taxes taken out on the 29th. Speaking of taxes, I did my own this year for the second time. I'm gonna get back $3000. You should get some pretty interesting stories from me while I'm in prison for this one. Remember that van I got from Vegas? I spent $500 on the chance that I could fix it myself. It only took $250 to get it working and I took the parts that I didn't use back for a refund. I charged it! Yep that's right I spent money. One charge card handled the whole thing. That is a good feeling. I actually gave myself a loan.

Yep! I just fixed the van, got the thing running great. Pulled it out of the storage unit, got about 100 feet before the thing started thinking on it's own. You would have thought somebody was controlling me by remote control. Transmission fluid clearly lead the way for the manager of the storage unit to find out who left that lake of oil on the cement. So much for saving money by fixing it myself! How much did I loose on this bright idea? Gotta visit the transmission shop, one day when it's in my budget.

If I'm not mistaken the interest on a credit card is much lower than those Check-into-Cash loan sharks. I figure it will be more comfortable living in the van than this Explorer. Eight credit cards totaling $6000. That is my total credit card debt and that is first on my list to pay off this year.

The jackrabbit never called me. I hate when people get my hopes up and don't follow thru. You know, Jim, the security guard manager. To hell with them, I hope a deceased camel sits in their French fires. I'm doing fine without em. They don't allow black people to have the extra hours anyway; they give all the extra hours to the white people.

I got an appointment next week to be a telephone-acting guy. Don't ask me, I don't know what that means all I know is that it's not sales and it pays $10 per hour to act on the telephone, wait till they get a load of me. Next week will tell the true story.

Got the van payments caught up but on the explorer, Ford still calls me at work regarding two payments late. Next week on the 15th is payday and two weeks after that I plan to be caught up.

Just ordered another drink, here she comes, my lady friend, gotta go.

Still looking for an extra job, I called a place I noticed on the Internet. Some sort of janitorial service was needed in Burbank. I saw a lot of jobs some paying from $9 to $15 per hour. I told the lady that my company was interest in doing the janitorial work for her office. She e-mails me back with more information on how to apply. The hours are perfect, a little hard work wouldn't hurt me, and I could create a janitorial company in

nothing flat. Strike up a crew of trust worthy
people and watch the money roll in. Besides,
$15 per hour would make it all worthwhile.
It's Ok to dream, but dreaming doesn't get you
out of debt.

"Hello, yes this is he", She's on the damn
phone; it's her, the woman from the Internet.
She called me and says it looks like it would
be a good gig for me. That I should call on
Monday and make an appointment with the rep.
"You do know about the MSDS don't you she
advises"? "O why yes of course the MSDS who
doesn't know about the MSDS. I love the MSDS"
I reply. CLICK! What the hell is the MSDS?
I drive 40 miles to the library in Burbank
as I was at my San Bernardino hang out at
the time. San Bernardino has a library but
it sucks as far as Internet access. You only
get one hour and no personal laptop access. I
arrive and get to work. It wasn't long before
I learned—Material Safety Data Sheets. It's
a frickin' way to inform you as to which
chemicals you should use for any given cleaning
situation. It's a safety net for employees so
you don't accidentally transform people into
powder after you're routine cleaning of the
company office.

The Internet says there is no professional
license needed to be a janitor but you need
this credential. Here we go, I'll make an
appointment for an interview on Monday but you
know what's going to happen when they see me.
They only hire white people. By the way, the
job is cleaning offices on the Warner Brothers
Studio.

He agreed to be fair. My boss, you know, the job interview for photographer. I told him that he had made a statement that I felt was unfair regarding being able to play a neutral roll when it came to selecting the best candidate for the position of Senior Photographer. He assured me that he could be fair. The interview went very well as I felt but you never know about these things. Two other people were on the board. Two very nice ladies who would be my bosses if I got the job, but what's the use? They only hire white people.

Another payday goes by, still late on one car payment. Unable to drive the van due to transmission problems but the engine runs great. I have gone back to check-into-cash and borrowed the maximum. Can't say when that will stop, I've said stop to many times before. Next week should be pretty interesting, Warner Bros. Says they may call me in for a second interview.

Just found out, the head of the photo unit just called me to advise me that I didn't get the job but we knew that.

Though I did think it very considerate of her to at least let me know what was going on. I didn't think to ask her the guy's race but we know, don't we. Maybe I should go and introduce myself after he gets settled in.

One job down, one to go, haven't heard from Warner Bros. Yet. Maybe sometime this week they will let me know. What am I talking about? They aren't going to tell me crap. They wouldn't do that; they just don't call you back. But then, we all know what's going to happen don't we.

Let's talk about money for a moment, after all that is what this book is all about. I truly sense that things are going to change this month, I mean for the better. For the last two paychecks I have noticed that I have my needs met, not if you count continuing to use check-into-cash. But things are smoothing out. I foresee a little extra cash in two weeks even after all the cars are caught up and all bills paid on time. The only regret I have this month is that I put $300 on a charge card for repairs thinking that I was going to be bedding down in the van. That didn't happen because it wasn't until I got the engine running in the van that I found out that the transmission was bad. But then you say how else could I have known. By the way, thanks for hanging in there with me. So odd thinking that one-day someone else may actually read these words poured from my brain.

I wonder if I will remember where these words were written I mean what exactly was my situation at the time. I'm sitting at work at my desk at LAPD Parker Center on Los Angeles Street on my lunch break. Hey Steve! Right now, visualize where you were when you said this. Man, are you stupid for writing this, who gives a damn about what you're going through? Everybody's going through something. What makes you think you're so special? Give it up, move in with a girl, have sex, pay half her rent. Don't you know how many girls would love to have you around? Almost out of debt Steve, she will tell her friends what a catch she made. "I caught this dude off the streets. He's got two jobs, he pays half the rent, buys the food and got three broke down cars, wow what a catch." STOP!

Slow down boy what the hell is wrong with you? Don't waste your lunch hour writing things like that. Please for give me for thinking like a wimp. Thirty thousand that's where I stand to date I can do this, I can do this . . . P.S. don't forget to visit a Chrysler dealer. Look at a car same year and model as yours, got to find out where those extra wires go on the engine I put back together.

Daughter sent me a letter yesterday. What's that got to do with finances you say? She was three years old when I left her and her mother. She found me through some Internet thingy called People Search. She wanted me to know that she is getting married. Twenty years later and I find out where she is when it's time to get married. Wait a minute—what the hell—married. Doesn't the father pick up the financial responsibilities for the wedding? What the hell is going on?

Speaking of what the hell is going on? I just got off the phone with my insurance company. They say that my son is sitting in front of them to get auto insurance. Yes, I did tell him when he got a car I would put him on my insurance but that was before I found out that my premium would go up $1800 a year to put a teenager on the policy. To hell and back with all this crap, I'm not praying for God to keep my kids healthy any more. What is going on? Do you know not a single person has asked me what I needed lately? I give up! Congratulations, you have arrived at the end of this book. Hope you enjoyed it! If you want your money back I understand. Let me conclude this book by saying. No body gets free from debt, if I couldn't do it no body can so stay right where you are, deep in debt, broke but low down debt cause they are not going to let you get free. Kids, neighbors, dogs, cats and goldfish, you're screwed buddy. If you're ever in the city of Pasadena, Burbank or Los Angeles look for the broke down Ford Explorer with the spray paint on the side that says "To Hell With You!" on it. Please walk softly when you pass by cause I'm inside, tired, broke all to hell, hungry and working two jobs. Get a life! THE END

Still here? Too bad for you, you could be living it up, spend all you have instead of reading this book. If you haven't returned the book yet—get this. I called my retirement office and informed them that I haven't received any word on the possibility of buying back time from two previous jobs. They gave me the old "you called us just in time" story. They were just about to send me the information that afternoon. Yeah right! They faxed me the information. It clearly stated that I was eligible to buy back four years of service. This means is that I would sign a contract to pay $500 per month for three years. This would increase my eligible retirement time enabling me to retire four years sooner.

Now as you may remember I just completed this process about two months ago. I paid almost $800 per month for three years, which gave me an additional ten years toward my retirement. To answer your question—I DID IT! I signed the contract allowing the city to take $500 per month for the next three years. Please don't be upset with me, yes I do want to get out of my car and live normal but take a look at the final out come. I have been working for the City of L.A. for only seven years. By doing the buy back thing, when all is said and done, I will have twenty-five years on the job and actually only worked for ten. I can retire from the city in three years. How many times in life are you offered the chance to regain lost years?

I don't know what will happen when these next three years are up, but I do know that the direction of life changes every day. To have gained the experience of living under my present conditions is not the norm yet has become acceptable, at least to me, a man who only wants to do right. Since the recent contact with my daughter I've come to realize that no matter what your situation, it is better to be prepared to help someone else. I live in this car and those who know about it think it's disgusting but God has shown be a way to survive.

This last episode with my retirement system has dulled my desire to expedite freedom. Something about knowing that there is no near freedom from living in my car keeps me moving at a steady pace. So much to living, and debt is a big part of it. In three years I'll be fifty-five, several financial changes will have taken place and some new from behind the

wheel reports will have evolved just for you,
I guarantee.

4/3/06—Got a call from Warner Bros. on Friday.
They said that my background check was complete
and they were offering me the job as casual
janitor as long as my references came back
clear. They will not be able to give me the
normal 8-hour orientation, which I would
greatly be interested in because you get paid
for the 8 hours. I will be working from 6pm to
2:30am Monday—Friday. We've been here before
right?

Two full time jobs, but at least this time I
can say I have an alternative motive. I'm gonna
learn everything I can about how films are made
and apply that knowledge to my productions.
Yes, I'm excited but I also realize that it
is a job, a job that has to be performed to
Warner's expectations to keep it. Also, I must
not show any signs of fatigue at LAPD. My
first night is tomorrow, it's true; the third
time is the charm.

I have applied to Warner Bros. on two other
occasions but failed for the same reasons.
They don't hire . . . Well they don't let
black people go to the 8-hour orientation.

I received an additional $300 this month in
the form of retroactive pay. This paycheck was
the no deductions check, which placed a total
of $2000 in my checking account. Every on
going bill I owe has been paid. Check-into-cash
was paid off and both car payments are paid
up. This huge opportunity has allowed me to
catch up on everything. Starting the second

job should bring about further opportunity to eliminate debt. At this point and time I'm about $30,000 in the hole.

The letter from IRS says my tax return refund of $2000 has been sent to the child support agency and applied to my past due account. That leaves me a grand total of $4000 due. At $500 per month it would be wise to pay them off ASAP. My son is now 15 years old. Another three years to go and no more child support. Don't get me wrong; I don't see my son as a financial relief. I see freedom from the system after he is 18. Only $300 actually goes to my ex-wife the other $200 goes toward late fees, principle, interest or whatever the child support agency wants to call theft. There is a long ways to go but this is the last year. I'm determined that this is the last year I am to be in debt.

4/5/06—The third day of employment with Warner Bros. It's damn hard work, I now have a greater respect for janitors. They started me out at $9.00 per hour and we get paid every week. I'm on vacation from LAPD so I will not feel the full repercussion of my new life style until next week. Time to get my chisel out and start figuring out what I should do with the extra money. Deep down I think I already know. Let the money from the City job keep the bills current. Use the money from Warner Bros. to chip away the rest of the bills starting with the smallest. Sounds like the war games are about to begin. Ladies and gentlemen of the jury, please allow me to exhibit my sum total financial responsibilities at this current time.

I put this note to show you my ingenious payment plan that calculates how long it will actually take me to get out of debt but the thing doesn't work. I'm still trying to figure it out myself.

4/7/06—I wasn't supposed to get a full on orientation. I learned that only permanent employees of Warner Bros. get the big orientation. I am in a so-called temporary position. When or if I become permanent I would also get a WB shirt to work in.

Please don't ask me how I did it but I checked my financial status yesterday and I am $450 over drawn. B of A sends the money to your automatic pay programmed creditor even though you don't have the money in the bank. Being on vacation I forgot to remember to transfer money from my savings account of LAPD Credit Union to the B of A checking account. That dumfounded act cost me $98 in Insufficient Funds fees. It's my fault, can't blame B of A but my thoughts now are that some of the money from the WB should always be channeled in the savings account as an overdraft protection. I really wanted to use the WB money strictly as a payoff method every week to knock out bills one at a time but I find I'm going to have to use it for catching up right now.

I joined the Entertainment Credit Union, which is located on the WB back lot. To my amazement upon inquiring as to becoming a member it was found that I was already a member. Some months ago in an effort to obtain a free lunch I joined the Entertainment Credit Union for a $5.00 special grand opening of their new building in Burbank. Little did I know that I was joining the Credit Union of my future employment? I sat up an automatic deduction of $50.00 per week. I wanted a nest egg and I think the credit union is a good idea.

Today marks the deadline for the application for the permanent position as janitor. I should know something next week. This permanent status would give me full benefits, retirement, paid holidays, medical and dental. I'm sure there is much more but I will only find out at the ORIENTATION.

CHAPTER 17

NO REGRETS FOR FRIENDSHIP

I feel rather sad; my friend read the pages of this book thus far. She's mentioned us going to a carnival. She feels somewhat disturbed that I would write information that related to the fact that maybe I shouldn't have used money toward my goal and decided to have some fun in life. You got to tell the truth about yourself. Not leading people on. I enjoyed spending time with her; sometimes there are people you are willing to give up your goal for. I needed you to know that a relationship, friendship or a total commitment has to be prioritized here.

Have no regrets for veering off course. A true friend is much more valuable than any goal you may introduce. This whole thing about saving, paying off and future obligations is based on one fact and one fact only. My staying alive long enough to enforce the very rules that I have incorporated for myself. If I were to die today what would all this be for? For naught, that's what, it seems to me that this entire plan is just in case I live to see it through and enjoy the fruits of the tree of persistence. Do I really understand what I am doing? Am I ready to sacrifice even that once and a lifetime relationship that seemingly floats across my path? I would like to blame it on past failures, pain that I have caused other relationships and not wanting to duplicate affecting another good woman in a negative way. But you can't live like that. You have to have some sort of relationship even if it is with yourself. As my friend told me, "If I were to try to do what you are doing, I would go stark raving crazy in about three weeks". You need someone who understands what you are trying to do in life. You need someone to tell you "don't give up, keep moving in what you believe in, I believe in you", the words which can only come from the inside.

Saw a black executive last night at Warner Bros. But we all know they don't hire blacks accept for janitors or putting them on the front line of the most dangerous job on the movie lot. Then again, wake up—it's a movie lot you know, actors and facades. Nothing is, as it seems on a movie back lot. I don't know why they would go through so much trouble to hire an actor on my shift just to make me think they hire blacks at the WB.

The first payday comes next Wednesday, gotta stay focused, stick to the plan pay off the first scheduled bill.

You ever wonder what in tar nations I'm going to do when the credit cards and cars are paid off? Well after that I pull another credit report through Operation Hope. I don't see the big advantage of being involved with them anymore but I do get free counseling on debt payment. Can't go to my last class on Thursday due to the new job at Warner Bros. I have inquired and can arrange to make an appointment to get the last class one on one. I should have graduated from that place months ago but there was no one to teach on real estate subjects, I would like to know how to buy a house.

Janitors are about to get a pay increase of 50 cents. This will include me but brings about an interesting question. Often times while working for LAPD I have had to film demonstrators protesting against this, that and the other. One of the largest and most known groups is called Janitors for Justice. This group is pounding the pavement twice a year and we (LAPD) are watching for any illegal activity with our cameras. It should be interesting the next time the janitors protest down the streets of L.A. what do I do? Now I'm one of them.

4/13/06—After receiving my first paycheck from Warner Bros. on yesterday, I took the check and traded it in for a money order. I addressed the envelope to my first creditor on the list and mailed it. First, minor goal accomplished. That pay off gave me a paid in full note and a $500 available credit limit on credit card #1.

One slight alteration in all this and I don't think I mentioned it before, the need to express love through financial action. With the recent reestablishment of the relationship with my daughter in Denver, I felt it necessary to break a few rules. Rules of change, changing the past: I'm finding that sometimes to build a better future it may take a little money especially when it involves long distances. Though I will have to get back to you after further study on the matter, I just sent my daughter Easter flowers. No not in my budget, no not preplanned but a simple gesture of faith. Her faith in me to do things that will make her happy, somehow, don't ask me why, it helps to shadow a darkened past when a material thought turns into a worthwhile investment like restoring my relationship.

Cancellation, that's what they say their gonna do. $545.00 is due in two days, so you may ask what has Steve gotten himself into now? Remember when I put my son on my car insurance so he could have a car to go to work and make money? At the time of the contract he agreed to pay his part. His part never came and here I am with the bill. What's a dad to do? Let the damn insurance cancel that's what! How the hell many times has he gotten paid since we signed the new contract? How many times did I hear he was driving to the mountains with his friends and sharing the cost of the hotel? I'm sorry folks, I'm sleeping in my damn car. Does anybody care? I know some people who don't, my kids.

Here's some new info I found out regarding auto insurance. Stay with me now you know how confusing I can get. Let me try to be simple as possible. As you know I own three cars two of which are stored in storage units and one of which I am still making payments of $400 per month. The one I'm paying on is out of order. But I still make payments and pay insurance on a car I can't use. Why you say? I did not know nor did the insurance company advise me that you do not have to make insurance payments on a vehicle that is out of commission. But you must have placed the vehicle in Non-op status with the DMV. Mercury Insurance has my

New Yorker, which by the way, has been paid off for several years as being leaned by the original finance co. This means that all this time I have been paying for car insurance on two vehicles that did not have to be insured. Just thought I'd let you know. I just found this out by trying to get other car insurance eliminating my son off my current policy. I ran into another problem along the way. The new insurance co. was unable to hold me to a contract because they need an address where the car I'm driving is going. They could not use my PO Mailbox.

This is going to be interesting when my present insurance cancels and then the finance companies will call and ask me why they are not insured. I will tell them that the insurance co. will not insure me because I don't have an address. Then they would ask me where the cars are housed and add their own insurance to my payments which is far more expensive.

All because of an agreement with my darling son; no returned calls, wild and wooly son. Let this be a lesson to him and me.

He is going to have to park the car and catch the bus to work. How soon we forget about how good we had it.

4/19/06—Second check from Warner Bros. has come I put it in the bank to save with the next check. This should be used to pay off Target and one of three Capitol One credit cards. I'm determined not to use any Warner Bros. money for anything but payoffs. If the check will not pay something off, it does not get used.

The $50 per paycheck still comes out automatically and goes into savings at the Entertainment Credit Union.

Got to be careful, I got a ding from the credit card bank last week. It seems I missed paying a credit card bill. They charged me $35 late fee. The silly thing about it is that the money was sitting in the bank, if I would only have paid more attention to my due dates on my statements I would have prevented this. I hate loosing money like that.

4/26/06—Just in the nick of time, like the governor calling to pardon the innocent man. My son calls me to give me the old phone wouldn't work excuse. He has $190 toward a $542 bill. He got paid today and says, "I'm already broke". What does it mean for a teenager to be broke? Does it mean that he has spent all his money on bills and such or that plans have already been make to spend weekends with friends with sports and concerts? What ever it is I feel another sweating session coming on when the bill is due. All and all it did save a lot of trouble being able to pay the premium rather than start all over again explaining my predicament and myself. I'll try to get the money out of him and save it for him myself if necessary so it wouldn't be so hard when the first payment comes in from the insurance company in about three months.

Payday from Warner Bros. tonight, the rest of the week should prove somewhat interesting as to what happens to it. I used the last Warner check of $200 toward the remaining balance of my son's insurance payment. I had believed that we were suppose to split the $545 bill but this morning the agent tells me that that was all the final bill of the additional car, Steve Jr.s car.

4/27/06—I did deposit the Warner Bros. check ($220) so this weekend I can sit down and take a good look at what should be paid off. Nice sounding words coming from a hobo. I remember not so long ago when I use to try to figure out which bill should be paid first, now as long as it's not over $400 I can pay it off. Not to mention an established savings account accumulating at $50 per week. The current balance is $100, it took the account the first check to become effective. Last night I overheard one of my co-workers tell someone that she didn't know where the $1000 she had made thus far at WB had gone. It made me think about something. Here is a lady that started working at WB on the exact date and time I did and she had no idea where her money had gone. I on the other hand can tell you exactly what I have done with every paycheck, which by the way totals the same amount. To me it's one thing to be exhausted for money that you are investing in yourself but I just don't think I could do this unless I could instantly see some tangible evidence of advancement in my life.

In case, you're still not quite sure exactly what I'm talking about, allow me to give you a rundown of my average day. Let's start with Monday. 3:00am I arrive at the Elysian Park Police academy. This is where I car pool with a co-worker and head to the Office at Parker Center downtown L.A. to do my video production

for LAPD. I'm off at 4:30pm. My car pool drops
me off back at the academy at about 4:50pm. Then
it's into my car and heading to Burbank. 5:15pm
I arrive at the Warner Bros. parking structure
gate #3. I change into my janitor uniform in
the car then check my alarm clock. I start
here at 6:00pm so my alarm is set for 5:45pm.
It only takes me 10 minutes to walk from the
parking structure through the back lot to the
building assigned for me to clean. After two
ten-minute breaks and a thirty-minute lunch
it's about 2:30am when all is said and done.
It's time to hit the road again; I'm headed to
the police academy at Elysian Park. I arrive
at 3:00am and hop in the shower change into my
video production clothes. 3:30pm I'm in my car,
I don't drive any where, I sleep in my car for
two hours. My alarm goes off at 5:30am giving
me a little time to get myself together before
the car pool arrives to start the process
all over again. This madness continues Monday
through Thursday. On Friday morning and 2:30am
when I get of from WB, it's to la la land
for me. I'm off every Friday from LAPD so I
don't have to be anywhere until the WB tonight
at 6:00pm which is my last shift before the
weekend. Please don't feel sorry for me it
gets better. When I get off at 2:30 from WB
on Saturday morning I am totally free until
the following Monday morning in which should
take you back to where you started reading my
schedule. In essence I'm looking at a total
of about 12 hours sleep from Monday through
Friday morning.

Allow me to throw in a curve for a moment. Of
all times the immigrants have decided to have
these silly demonstrations through out the

cities protesting immigration reform. This puts me on a rotating list to work on any given Saturday and/or Sunday to photograph and demonstrations or protests that occur in LA. Just keep in mind the schedule we just discussed and add 5 hours on Saturday and 5 hours on Sunday working the crowd. You're right, seven days a week for now, there is no time off. But something has got to give.

One inspiration and one inspiration only, each Wednesday night is payday and another bill is paid off and that puts me closer to being totally out of debt then I can stop writing this stupid book. Then the fun begins, I purchase equipment to work my dreams. The plays, films, television shows and . . . Okay maybe another book. But somewhere in the back of my mind I can't help thinking about my purpose. I mean why a man with such determination to purchase production equipment would somehow end up working at one of the worlds greatest facilities specializing in the very same thing. Oh well, my lunch at LAPD is over and my eye are very heavy. Just a few more hours to go, remember? It's Thursday so this begins my weekend when I get off at 2:30am from WB.

4/30/06—Two more down four to go, credit cards that is. A total of four credit cards have been paid off since I started the Warner Bros. plan three weeks ago. As you probably guessed, since I only take home $220 per week, that would mean that each balance on the counts was under $220. This is correct but this get steeper. My next pay off balance is $480 in which I will have to accumulate Warner pay, about three weeks, before I can pay off this amount. All

and all my total credit card balance is about
$5000. This equals out to about 25 weeks but
that concludes only the credit card debt. Note
that the money I'm using to pay off these debts
comes from my additional funds, the Warner
money. This would mean that the LAPD money
should increase. Not having to pay out funds
from this income should leave more from that
account. Don't worry I didn't understand that
myself.

After the credit cards are gone it looks like
the cars are next. by the way, did I tell
you that the state finally figured out a way
to attach your State taxes on to your child
support payments? No big deal, it all gets paid
and they do have a huge interest and penalty
rate. My balance with child support for back
support was $6000 two weeks ago. At this time
I owe $3000 because of the funds from my tax
return. If I were to pay this account off in
full it would add $285 a month to my available
money. It looks like with a total such as this
the child support balance should be paid off
after the credit cards are said and done.

There's a long ways to go but I'll tell you
something. To be able to see on weekly basis
the difference in my financial plan sure eases
the pain of the night shift.

5/6/06—Sure feels good! Statement of the first
paid off credit card arrived today. Account
paid off, $500 credit limit and balance of—45
cents. The negative sign indicates that
they owe me money. At this time ladies and
gentlemen I would like to take just a moment

to discontinue my writings, I seem to feel a
tear coming on . . .

Thank you! Still somewhat blurry eyed let me
find my place. I begin the payoff the lowest
balance credit card but as you probably figured,
the remaining credit cards go up in balance. I
choose to start with the lesser balances so I
could instantly get some gratification. Card
#4 has a balance of $475. It will take me three
weeks to pay this account of. By the way Warner
Bros. contacted me this week. They offered me
permanent status as janitor, I accepted. A new
job opening came up at LAPD its called Police
Surveillance Specialist. As far as I can tell
I qualify. It starts off at $6,000 per year
more than I currently make as an audiovisual
technician. I'm going for it but as you know
they probably don't hire black people. Where
was I? Credit card #5 has a current balance
of $650, #6 is $820, #7 is $865, #8 is 867
and credit card #9 has a balance of $1810.
I estimate that if I follow through with my
plan as I have been, all cards will be paid
off in six months. My plan is at that time to
start paying off a #3800 back child support
balance. Still can't get the other cars in
my storage fixed, not in the budget. I can't
get too excited for there is darkness in the
myths. My department manager with LAPD came to
me the other day confidentially; he said that
he heard some whispering from the fort office
regarding the work permit I had submitted for
the Warner Bros. Job. They asked him how many
hours per week I am working for the WB? He
said he didn't know. The rules are that you
cannot work more than 20 hours per week while
working on another job while working for LAPD.

You folks know me pretty well by now, wouldn't that be a shame if I had to quit Warner? I pray that the signed document from the head officer in charge comes to me confirming the approval of my work permit. Isn't that how it happens. People everyday lie, cheat and deceive to gain their objective but people like you and me, those how believe in truth and just being who you are usually end up getting scrutinized for our integrity. But you know I've found in life that despite all the negative that may come your way when you just do right, I always feel better about myself no matter what the out come. Gotta go now! I have an application to fill out.

P.S. A Police Surveillance Specialist is the guy who wires cops who are going under cover and record other people making bad deals.

5/21/06—Some interesting stuff to report this time. Strange letter arrived from a credit card bank. They say $55 is being mailed to me, evidently when I applied for the card about five years ago I was required to put a $55 deposit in the account. This happens to be one of the accounts now paid off through the Janitor plan. Also got a letter from another paid off account that said, "Please don't send any more money to this account". Can ya get to that? When you owe a credit card monster money they want it when they say and with interest. In this case the account is paid in full and I am still making payments toward the account. Now they owe me money and are freaking out. I want to see what happens to the money to the money when the statement comes are they going to send me back the money every month, increase my limit or close the account this should be interesting. The other three accounts that are now paid in full have accepted the additional payments and have given me a credit toward that amount.

Car insurance sent me $45 because of the change I made in my policy, as you may recall I advised them that two of the three cars were out of service. I do fell somewhat stupid due to the fact that I have been paying on these vehicles for several years and could have been saving much more money. Once again and almost two paychecks later my son has not contacted me regarding his portion of the car insurance payment. But I'm the dad, he's only 19 years old, he needs your help Steve! Well he's working full time, living at home with his mother, quit school and the car he is driving was a gift from one of his friend's parents as long as he maintained full coverage. In other words his only obligation is . . . lets see now . . . I just can't seem to think of anything. So the insurance is due on the 22nd of next month. I'm going to find out the last day before I receive the new bill and that will be the day I take him off my policy. Yeap! I'm the dad.

One switch-a-rue in my pay off plan for the final four credit cards, I remember some time ago talking to a friend regarding which credit cards to pay off first. He stated, "Pay off the card with the highest interest". After close review of my accounts Sears wins the lottery coming in at 29%. The next three accounts come in at 26%, 22% and 21%. Last week was the first time that I did not pay off an account;

I deposited the money and will do so until the balance of the Sears account is saved up.

This should take three more weeks at $200 a pop. In other words my current balance with Sears is about $800.

My original thinking was to pay off the lowest balance first, I am passing up a lower balance to pay off the highest interest account and I hope I'm doing the right thing.

Things going quite smoothly at Warner Bros. Every morning at 2:30 I still walk the back lot gazing at all the buildings mentally lining up my shots. So quiet, so serine, thinking on the day when I'll be out of debt and using my own equipment to make these images in my head come to life. I never quit writing during this process. Television, radio, film, sitcoms bouncing around in my head then to paper. The only time I have to write is on lunch breaks and weekends. I watched two films being made recently. 'De Ja Vu' starring Denzel Washington. And I have the honor walking through the carnival scene of Nenimits (I think that's the name) staring Eddie Murphy. I just spoke to another friend who told me that the plan about paying off the highest interest first is stupid so I'm switching back to paying off the lowest balance first.

I don't really spend a lot of time in my car anymore since I started working the night job at Warner. There is not much time to sleep except on the weekends. I actually seem to be getting use to the job. I've learned to pace myself and rest on lunches and breaks. Time goes by so slowly but when you compare waiting three or four weeks to pay off a credit card that would have cost you three or four times the original balance when paid three or four years, it makes it all worth while.

6/16/06—Been paying the critters every week since the last entry. Working five days a week Monday thru Friday on 3 or 4 hours of sleep per day for the last three months. I must say this has been the millstone stumper of my goal but I must also admit that my body is starting to do some strange things. My immune system is showing signs of fatigue and just in the last few days I am experiencing slight headaches. I feel saddened that I may have to relinquish my superman mentality just to survive but I will give it another week just in case it's hopefully just a bug. It's not only the human side of me that will be disappointed it's the creative side of me. Knowing that I will no longer walk down the streets of the back lot of my dreams. All the movies I produced in my head while visualizing myself singing in therein. How many times have I directed my own movie in the shadows of those unoccupied neighborhoods and sound stages. I even wrote a teleplay with those structures in mind. I haven't finished it yet but it's called "less than a Whisper". Written about ad within the Warner back lot.

Needles to say at $200 per week over the last three months I have done some great damage to my debt in fact this week alone I was able to pay off not one but two bills and one of them was the previously mentioned Nix Check Cashing. I originally owed them $300 but after not paying them for not paying them for almost three years the total I gave the last night was $449. I will soon receive a letter of pay off and t this infraction taken off my credit report. I started this entire venture with a FICA score of about 500. That was almost a year ago, I will soon be pulling another report and let you know what it is now. I some feel as if I've let you down by possibly having to let Warner Bros. go due to health reasons.

6/29/06—Still hanging in there. Three more WB checks and Sears is history. Couldn't bring myself to leave just yet, Warner Bros. that is. Very, very tired but it's full speed ahead.

7/1/06—I talked to my friend today about life. I told her how I thought that I had failed in life financially. That if only I'd had known what I know now; 'if only', was the sum total of my conversation. She replied, "me too".

7/4/06—Gonna have to hold off on the idea of paying off Sears for a minute. Packing thing up for tonight, look out Pasadena, it's off to the Rose Bowl with plenty of food and drinks. Went to Costco and left a $200 tip yesterday. Have you ever known me to splurge? Okay so your new word of wisdom at this point is to only splurge on Holidays. Yelp! That's the new rule, only on Holidays. All kidding aside, lets look a little deeper at this splurge thing. The money was there did you get that? The money to splurge was just sitting in the bank and no bills will suffer from the splurge. What I'm saying is, to be in a position to spend a couple hundred dollars and not have it effect anything but maybe postpone your goal for a week, that's good financial planning. Gonna pick up my girl in San Bernardino and head for a 4th of July boat ride in San Pedro and all the fresh fish we can eat then look out Pasadena, it's off the Rose . . . wait a minute—isn't this where I started?

7/14/06—Sears received its first payment of $100. This will occur for 6 weeks. I will have two more credit cards left after that but they are the big ones. Met a couple of people talking about financial planning. I've been checking the net for financial planning software. I figure if it's easy enough to operate I can pay the $40 to purchase the software rather than the $40 per hour to talk to a professional. I only have one bad boy to report this session. I charged $450 to one of the cards that was paid off. Here's what happened. On August 8th 2006 my auto insurance premium is due. The cost is to be $1700 paid in increments of $380 per month. By the way I should mention that my auto insurance is currently with Mercury. Well, just the other day I was watching the news and they stated that AAA was signing it's policies not according to your zip code but by your driving record. Yesterday I paid AAA a little visit. Long story short, I gave myself a loan and started with the AAA plan. I also became a member in the process. I will be saving $500 a year by transferring over to AAA. In essence I gave myself a loan and scheduled myself to pay myself back within 30 days.

7/21/06—University of Phoenix is history. Paid the balance on my student loan. This balance was also keeping me from continuing my education. For you UOP students keep track of how your money is being spent. UOP allowed me to continue taking classes even though Wells Fargo had stopped paying them. I was yanked from school having to pay off my last two classes out of pocket. It took me two years, but this is the account I paid off today. Taking a look at things thus far, I for see still being on driving myself out of debt into next year. I for see all debts paid accept the two cars. The ford is estimated at a $6000 balance and the Chrysler at $9000. If I'm still at the WB, I will have $4000 per month to apply to these loans.

7/23/06—I found it! I remembered some years ago when I first started this get out of debt thing; I had purchased a book titled "Credit Report" by Leonard & Loonin. I read it and put it in storage. Thinking now it's time to take a real good look at my credit report, I decided to dig it out. It says that it's time for me to start writing letters to the credit reporting agencies regarding discrepancies on my report. Got the letters done and sill send them as soon as I print them out tomorrow. I counted at least 14 discrepancies on my credit report, we will see what reporting agencies have to say after they get a load of me.

CHAPTER 18

ANOTHER SETBACK

6/31/06—Set back in progress. Just received a letter from IRS. They say I cannot use the car payment to my ex-wife as a deduction, called alimony and claimed for the year of 2004 and want $1700 in 30 days. OK, so I was wrong to think that just because the car payment is court ordered that I could deduct it as alimony. I went to my tax program, (TaxAct) and recalculated my taxes without the so-called alimony deduction. It only came to $900 not $1700. I will send IRS a copy of my recalculated form and a letter explaining why I thought what I did. It was because when I sent my calculations they gave me the money owed to me. That's why I thought it was okay to use the same deduction in the year 2005. At least I know what's in store for me next year. I can start saving for it now.

You knew didn't you, you knew when you heard me say that I was deducting the car payment on my taxes that it wasn't going to work. Do me a favor, the next time you read that I am going to make a mistake, please tell me before the next chapter.

8/6/06—What a brainstorm, yeah right! Well, I did it again, became another statistical example of what Webster defines as STUPID! At this time I am ending this book in which I will quickly explain and allow you to get on with your lives. I do apologize for those of you I am leaving out in the cold just sitting in your car anticipating the day you are debt free but I can no longer be considered an example to follow. As you may recall, I have these three vehicles. Well, just let me refresh your memory regarding my vehicle situation. I have a 1992 Chrysler, paid for but with a broken radiator. I have one 1998 Ford Explorer I use for all driving with a balance of $6500 and one un-drivable 2000 Chrysler Town and Country with a $3000 repair estimate, in a storage unit. Anyway, I say to myself, trade in the Explorer with the 110 thousand miles on it along with the Broken Town and Country. That way you can have an extra $500 from the Explorer payment, $165 from the storage unit and as long as the payments on the new car are under $650 per month you come out ahead. So I take my brain down to the car dealer and explain my dilemma. They were so kind to help me get my finances together. To make a long story short, I drove out of the parking lot with a brand new Chrysler Town and Country and only a $600 per month payment. I smiled all the way down the street as I watch the odometer turn to its first 7 mile mark. By the way, I was able to retrieve my credit report the car dealer pulled to check my history. About one year ago my FICO score was 500. Last weekend I was at 640 so you really can up your score using common since but now the kind that comes from this book for you see at about mile 8 on my odometer I realized that I still have the broken Town and Country that I'm paying $400 per month on. I still have the storage unit that I'm paying $165 per month to store the Town and Country and now I'm paying $600 per month for the new car with a balance or $40,000 if I pay as agreed. I just wanted a bigger more comfortable car to live in. Therefore, I conclude this book and thank you for your reading but with my new 72 month contract and IRS on my ass there is no since in kidding myself, I am no good example. Hope you come out better than I, have a good in life!

8/9/06 2:21pm—Received a phone call from my 25 year old daughter's attorney. "Hello is this Mr. Steven Sloan? My name is so-and-so, I'm calling in regards to a child support court order for the year of 1985. I'm calling to collect a total including principles and interest in the amount of $85,000. This guy was really hard pressed to offer me a deal of 50 cents on the dollar. Have you ever heard of the child support agency offering a deal like that? I think I'll give the agency I am currently paying a call and try to work out a deal anyway, at this point this is where people usually become a statistic and you read about them the next day. The fact of the matter is, there is a court ordered child support judgment against me in 1985 but when my ex-wife took all my retirement in the tune of approximately 28,000 I just figured we were even Steven. Why didn't the man on the phone mention that fact? The saga continues . . .

8/18/06—I pick up letter from post office box. The details regarding my court ordered child support are there but no details regarding payment options. Contacted 'Dad's Law' attorney who wants $150 for the first hour of consultation. I would much rather spend that $150 toward my first payment. What can the attorney tell me to do? The only thing that bothers me is why didn't my daughter's attorney send the payment options offered me on the phone in writing? The $.50 on the dollar motion, why he didn't even send me his card or phone number, nothing; the only thing in the envelope I received was my original divorce decree. I know there is no statute of limitation in my case but I can't help but think that something still just doesn't feel right. I saved his call back number the day the attorney contacted me and I will call the beginning of next week to advise his that I need more information to take to my attorney. In the back of my mind I sense I want to tell this guy that I could never come up with his $40,000 proposal and to go ahead with the city's court ordered distribution but this may sound like I'm giving him the go ahead to automatically deduct the money from my paycheck. Anyway, this affects my dreams for a while. I've broken my own cardinal rule; never allow your debts to force you into becoming obligated to your second source of income. In other words, always be in a position where you can quit your extra income source with out jeopardizing any financial obligations.

I have revised my payment schedule three times this week and will contact my daughter's attorney to arrange payments. No answer in the attorney's office left message that I did not have $40,000 and inquired as to when the city of L.A. would begin deductions. I found an attorney especially made for child support dads but they wanted $150 per hour. One thing I'm still puzzled about. Why didn't my ex-wife just go through the courts and take the money. That seems easier than hiring a company from

out of state to handle me. The courts would
have taken the money every two weeks for the
next 18 years, that's how long I figure it will
take me to pay it off. I will be 70 years old
when and if this account is paid off. Valaugh!
That's it, could it be that the courts cannot
offer settlements but outside sources can. And
who about the deadbeat dad not surviving past
age 60 or so. If I died before the 18 years
were up the money would be cut off. Or would
it? Anyway I'll tell ya what. Hope the girls
enjoy the money cause come October this year my
insurances are due for review. I can make any
changes at that time and the first change I'm
going to make is to take my daughter flat off
any beneficiary documents I have. And should
I die before that time let this letter serve
notice that all my monies go to my son Steven
Eric Sloan Jr. and Daniel Arron Sloan. All
of you millions of people reading this book,
don't let them give anything to her . . . not a
squat nickel. Oh no you got it all wrong, I'm
not upset that I have to take on a new child
support obligation after almost 30 years. She
could call me a few months ago, she wrote me
letters initially, you can't tell me they don't
know how to get in touch with me yet nobody
bothered to contact me to discuss this matter.
Some people just can't face you when they are
stabbing you in the back. Wrong again, I'm not
angry that the whole purpose of the contact
and all that forgive and forget, all that
ending her letter with dad and every thing is
fine now crap. IT WAS A SET UP! Can't you see?
Every notion was to obtain information, which
would end up in the kill. Heaven knows why I
never got-up enough courage to tell her that

I'm homeless, sleeping in my car. Who would believe me know?

I sent out the IRS letter explaining that I would start payments on September 15th.

10/4/06—What do you mean I forgot to sign the form? So my payments didn't start on time, how could I have been so careless? I resent the papers to start my payments on the 18th so October.

I've been married exactly one month today. Meeting Cynthia would have done me better if I would have met her before I moved into my car but I'm sure things happen for a reason. Combining our money is working out just fine. We have already looked into real estate. The plan to continue the out of debt goal is still a priority in our lives. At this time we are a total of $50,000 in debt. She drives the new car, I inherited her old maxima out the deal which by the way is in need of repair so that makes two broke down cars I have is storage. I'm still with Warner Bros. five days a week so that gives us only three days a week together. Our apartment is in San Bernardino where Cynthia works as a caseworker for the County of San Bernardino. My work schedule only allows me to go home on the weekends. She so understands, I guess that's why it's so easy to do for her. I try to budget $100 per week just for "doing together money". I'm looking for another job in San Bernardino so I can be with my wife at nights. Cynthia was well aware of my original plans when I was sleeping in my car and is willing to do the same thing but at $800 per month for our one bedroom apartment we can still do a lot of damage to our finances it will just take a little longer to get out of debt.

10/15/06—No more paying off anything, just keep your cool and hold on tight. My new wife and I are doing fine. I handle the finances and every time I mess up she totally understands. I'm not paying off anything any more but I am doubling up the requested payments from credit cards. I think I made a mistake but I'm not sure. If I didn't mention it earlier, some time ago I found in a thrift store a movie dolly. This thing was built in the early 1900s and is a moviemaker's antique dream. The three hundred pound four-wheeled piece of history was $2000. I also found an editing machine, if you know what I'm talking about, for $1000. Deep in all my debt I offered the owner $1500 for the both of them. We agreed to $300 down and $300 per month for the next four months. I spoke to my wife about it and she was so cool. She says that she knows that I would only do the best for the both of us. I guess that's why I feel so convicted about spending the money. Our third car needs $600 worth of work and my old van needs $3000 work and here I go spending this money on a dream. I guess I better figure out how to make it right by renting the equipment out to movie studios for that 1930s movie making look.

12/27/06—A wonderful Christmas day with my wife: All bills are on time; the new van was refinanced for a lower interest rate. The plan is to quit WB in two weeks and start focusing on the business (Fountain of Life Productions). About $1000 has been spent in equipment over the past few months $700 was made in Las Vegas working on a show. She pushes me to get the business going.

An office and studio now occupy our apartment. We are now are in a position that I maintain all bills, accept rent. Her paycheck is used to pay off a debt $800 or less. At this rate the projected time of OOD (Out Of Debt) is two years. Cynthia had several past obligations on the back burner that had gone to collections but they have all been brought to the surface and if not paid off we are now dealing with on a monthly pay plan. The van in storage is still broke, never saw it in the budget to get it fixed and I still owe $10,000 on it. We have obtained a tax identification number and business charge card. Upon opening a checking account for the business we got a secured card to establish credit in the company name.

1-6-07—It's final, WB is history. I resigned yesterday and now comes the challenge of faith. Switching my focus on the business my wife and I are starting. Video production (with no cameras), Audio production (with no microphones) it should be a very interesting adventure. All we really have is each other. Gotta start thinking about getting the receipts together for tax time. Just in case this turns out to be something—I retrieved all my original music disks from storage yesterday and am in the process of selecting songs to complete for recording projects. Still able to pay off debt! Paid off wife's dental bill of $800 last month and project paying off others next month. Loosing WB is going to effect things a bit but gotta find a way to make up the difference in what comes natural.

CHAPTER 19

BACK TO SCHOOL

7-11-07—A new inspiration directs me back to reality. First, day of school, I've been wanting to finish my degree for years but had to pay off a few things first. The instructor says start a journal. This is my cue to restart and continue where I left off. A lot has happened since my last entry. I started teaching acting at John Robert Powers Acting School. Advanced commercial and the audition. The students loved it as much as I did. We filmed every Saturday and produced our own sit-come called The Untamed Attic. I don't know what gives me the right to think that I could change someone's life for the better but they sure paid attention. Last Saturday was the last of a ten-week course. We had a screening so all the parents could see what they were paying for. I saw people change portions of their lives all because of something I said. I had an idea in my mind and I watched people who didn't even know me do exactly what I told them to and believe what I said was true, willingly.

7-12-07—Opening my eyes my head first pointed almost instinctively toward the clock. Yips! I over slept. Necked before I hit the bathroom door I hop in. My wife doesn't understand how I get by with so little sleep. It's off to work I go. Still driving from San Bernardino to Los Angeles each day. My new class is wonderful. My instructor suggests that we search our souls for inspiration from the world around us. Why are my thought so scattered with all these films in my head. What do I do with these images? Will I ever get to produce them? Should I film them as shorts? Talking into my mini cassette more often than usual. It comes in spurts like labor pains. Here it comes again.

This is a story about a very creative man with abdominal pains. He unbearably makes it home from work. Crawling to his desk he picks up his cassette player and very painfully speaking into the microphone gives birth to his ideas which turn into movie trailers, films, skits and plays.

7-13-07—a very special place in life, that's what I hold. How satisfying to be doing what you love to do. Filming—thinking your last name is Spielberg. We looked at the camera for the first time. The image for the day was being lost, lost in a strange world. The parking lot filled with confusion. Which way do I go? I search through the forest of cars to finally find the security office that allows me to purchase my parking pass for school. Suddenly the parking lot is not so bad.

7-14-07—The corner of the pillow was the first thing I saw this morning but my first thought was to do something for class so here it is. My wife has problems sometimes recognizing if what I talk about is coming from my present world or if I'm describing a new film scene so . . . we've come to an agreement. Whenever I am going to speak on a subject that is in my vision, I simply say "In the Sloan world" prior to the explanation and she knows that what she is about to hear is either the making of a film, play or song, at least some that does not as of yet exist. Just in case you're wondering, we are still on a financial goal toward debt relief. I do recognize by now that the purpose in getting out of debt is to establish a new debt. Once we recognize that it make it easier when things don't quite go as planned. How about that! Plan the way you get in debt, I guess it makes since if you have to be in debt be in it on your own terms. That gray van (Big Gray) that was in storage for so long, man, is it a blessing. Still paying the credit cards off for the new transmission but I think we made the right move. The wife drives the new car (Little Gray) and her old car (Little Blue) took the parking place in the storage unit. It just needs $400 work to fix a major oil leak. And then there's Louise, my 1992 Chrysler New Yorker. On occasion I have had to use Louise while Big gray was in the shop. Please allow me to leave you with a mental note here. It's a fact that teaching is in me. One of my current students is also an instructor at the school (Art Institute). When I asked him what he wanted to do in life he stated that he is doing it. He wants to retire as a teacher at the school. I think that is what I would like to do also.

7-15-07—She feeds off of my imagination. Sometimes I think that what really makes her happy is when I tell her what's on my mind. Somehow she can see in my eyes when I'm in Sloan's world. That place where very few can see, so she asks me what I'm thinking about and sets back to enjoy the ride. Did you know that there are movie viewers who totally engulf themselves in what they are experiencing at the time? I never knew that until I met Cynthia. Her focus is so precise that even when she reads a book you may find that she leaps to her feet from the sound of a shot fired on the next page. My vision today is having her near me, to read all that I write, to see all I produce and to be part of all that I have.

7-15-07—DEBT what we all desire to be free from: It's important that we all achieve financial stability. The responsibility must be handled with every intention to alleviate the stress that accompanies debt, but there must be a happy medium that always comes to the surface. Sharing the responsibility and recognizing debts short comings and advancements. For instance, my wife has wanted for some time now to have the carpet cleaned. That happened this weekend. The nails, hair and make-up must all be included in the plan. One piece of the financial pie is dedicated to what she needs to be happy. Without this intention the plan becomes a burden and is likely to fail. So remember as you execute your plan to get out of debt that you include that significant other as one of the obligations in order to succeed.

7-16-07 IDEA—12 midnight and all is well. Can't sleep, went to bed too early. My vision statement seems to lead me to my very surroundings. What I mean is that ever since my wife and I filmed at our apartment complex, those areas now become more than just areas. The designated spots I chose as locations for filming now seem to stick out each time I pass them by. I find that true in the cityscapes of Los Angeles also. Having been on the set of

several films now added to my library, those
spots in the city that were used to film tend
to stand out in my mind when I pass by those
very places where I witnessed all the lights
and confusion.

CHAPTER 20

STARTING ALL OVER AGAIN

DRIVING—This Wednesday marks only the second installment in a new one year goal to get out of debt. The plan is set up to where the paycheck issued to my wife on the 15th will be used to pay off something. According to plan that something is whatever bills equal up to $800. Last month was the first installment. We seem to be in a position of catch up at this time. In other words simply making ends meet. I have placed my prediction on a calendar in anticipation of paying off and will let you know how things came out. Let me add this one note. According to what I hear from authorities regarding the average finical obligation, if a person even has $800 extra per month to apply to the liquidation of debt, they are considered extra ordinary. Not to brag but I want to place it in my own mind that, no matter how hard you plan or whatever tactics are used in an effort to get out of debt. Your plan is always succeeding when your needs are met and those who depend on you for support indicate that they are happy. When you can confess to this, being out of debt is simply a fringe benefit.

7-17-07—IDEA—An odd observation regarding my vision statement. While driving down a business area looking for an image for class I started reading the business signs along the way. I found it humorous when I started reading all the signs and billboards as one entire sentence

as I passed a donut shop, tire repair and
billboard. "Always hot and delicious, Joe's
Tires, or you can order on line.

DEBT—Does school add to the problem? The credit
card I used to get started in school had a
balance of $50. The new bill just came leaving
me a balance of $494 on a $500 limit. Not to
mention a new school loan of $89,000 for a
person who feels so strongly about getting out
of debt. No excuses—this is just my thinking for
now. The road for opportunity and promotion,
at least for a black man, is paved for the
most part by matching education, knowledge
and experience with those in competition with
today's social efforts. To place myself in a
position to where the additional funds needed
only need make a decision on my work ethics,
integrity and attitude working with others
would be of great advantage to me. On the
negative note, yes, I spiral my family down the
tunnel of further financial obligation. Might
I add at this point that the idea of getting
a BS was discussed and approved by all family
members involved. My current school loan of
$89 per month will be notified and will stop
coming but that does not release me of the
obligation. Therefore, despite the offer to
discontinue making payments the payments will
continue as scheduled. In only my first week
of school, now is the time to start thinking
about how to repay the new loan. I'm not
saying allow the money to distract me just be
perfectly aware that every month I'm in school
I'm adding $1000 to my debt obligation. This
works on me in several ways. Sure makes me
want to keep up my grades and look for ways to

promote while in school to take up the slack when I get out and it's time to pay the bill.

One mention here, on yesterday I received a call from Los Angeles Personnel Department. They have scheduled an appointment for an interview for the position of Video Technician. This job will add $3000 a year toward my school loan payoff and open a door for promotion down the line. If I haven't stated this before, I have been at my maximum for the past year and there are no promotional steps in my class or category. I have to leave LAPD Audio Visual Department to advance financially and compete for promotional opportunity. My interview is July 24th, wish me luck!

7-18-07 Once again the alarm clock seems larger than normal as it captures my eye as the first image of the day. Up and at it got to check my homework for class this morning. Three or four more years of school, so I have to figure out a way to have my cake and eat it too. How to make films and keep up with my classes? Can I do it? An acquaintance from Las Vegas called me yesterday. He didn't want anything particular just to let me know what he has been doing with his craft. He says he is getting ready for the 48-hour film festival. I couldn't wait to check it out. This now becomes my vision statement for the day. I think I'll switch over to the internet for a moment and check out the subject, I'll be right back. Too Late! The competition was last month. But I did not miss the festival itself. This Saturday at the Fine Arts Theater, we will be there.

DEBT—I guess the above statement doesn't look to good. Trying to get out of debt and all but taking my wife to some silly film festival. How about this—I need to go to film festivals so I can see how they are done. This will impart the much necessary knowledge and skill to my wife and I, as to how to enter and submit our own films, which in turn give us additional income to spend on bills when we win the contests. How's that?

7-21-07—Everything is paid on time including the unexpected. You know, those things that just seem to come out of nowhere, like the car registration, annual insurance payment . . . And that my friend is why we cannot complete our payoff goal. The car insurance is automatically deducted each month for 9 months. After that, for three months it only feels like you paid something off. Got to hold off on paying union dues and the least amount credit card until I see another break.

IDEA—Today started off with a song. Its hard at 4am to keep it down as not to wake the neighbors. Not about anything particular just to know I've still got it. The wife is drawn to the music and lies on the sofa to allow me to score her most intimate dream. Still have plans to go to the film festival tonight. This will be the first one for us. I noticed the entry fee for this show was almost $200 per film. It will be interesting to see what a filmmaker deems to be the worth so his trouble. Most importantly, we are going to see how we stand in the independent world. Would one of our films have been capable of standing next to these or better yet, if we would have know about the festival would we have invested in the same way?

7-22-07—IDEA—Not what I'd expected. The film festival at the Fine Arts Theater was jam-packed. The 48 Hour Project sponsored its Los Angeles Film Festival. Sorry to say my wife and I didn't even stick around to see who won. Disappointed that very few if any knew how to tell a story. These were images in someone's mind that were previously thought out and included in the production. But maybe it was because of the rules: One Prop, One line and 48 hours to produce a 5-7 minute film and everything must be created within that time. The reason I say that the contestants had pre-conceived props and gags is because at times the movie didn't make sense. The show lasted about two hours and with each new film, the audience roared. One aspect on the film I thoroughly enjoyed was watching the films and seeing the actors sitting right there next or just in front of you. All in all it was truly an experience that I needed to see. If anything, it showed me that I'm not so bad of a filmmaker. Or shall we wait until next years 48 hour project to see just where I stand.

7-22-07—DRIVING—Why? do I feel so self-conscious about the $50 lunch. We had such a wonderful time together, my wife and I. arriving into Pasadena for the class reunion we found ourselves famished. A quick stop at a familiar place and the credit card gets lubricated. The discussion to move closer to our jobs come into play as to how much money we would save, at the present we spend $500 per month on gasoline. Has it come to that point in our society? We have to consider so much these days if we want to at least live our lives where there is no one chasing us down to collect a payment due. No regrets, if you can sit down and laugh with someone you love and save enough money to do it again, you're in a better position than you know.

IDEA—If I were offered the chance to go back in time to my high school years and relive my life, would I do it? I don't think so was my reply. This was just one of the many questions my wife asked me yesterday at my 35th high school reunion picnic. But in actuality I did go back in time several times. Seeing my classmates, I couldn't help but think about certain situations reflecting back in the day. The days we walked for miles marching through the streets and grass soaked with morning dew practicing for a game or competition. What impressed me most was the fact that so many people recognized me. There were very few whom I remembered who they were. Those were the ones who I was in classes with and had very little personal contact but those whom I remembered most were the members of the John Muir High School Mighty Mustang Drum Section. All three years of my High School days were spent as a drummer. I often wondered if I still had what it takes to swing those mighty drum sticks for hours at a time and yesterday was my proving ground. On my wife's suggestion, I through your drum in the back of the car, just in case". Just in case was the very thing that happened. Man, did we play, all the cadences just started rolling back to my memory. Though sometimes waiting for a few beats to pass before I joined in did help to jog my memory. With my wife on camera and my mind back in 1972, I was involved in a practical application in a blast from the past, can't wait to see the footage.

7-28-07 Driving—Just send me your address and I'll send you all the money I intend to throw away. Just left the bank with my wife. Transferred $100 from her account into mine, somehow, don't ask me how, I miscalculated the account for bills and am now in need of her services. I lost $45 dollars in over draft fees, I should have been watching the account closer. Believe me, if you're not watching your account, the bank is. On the positive side, the wife and I just came from the store and bought 61 dollars in food, filled up the tank. We did it with money the bank owed us. By over paying the account gives us a credit card savings account. I just wish I would pay attention enough to keep that extra money in the bill paying account so I could avoid giving it away.

Idea Journal—My greatest fear is fear itself. Specifically told not to be afraid to face my issues I still reserve some anticipation of this coming Monday. You see, the guys and I at work had an in depth meeting regarding how difficult it is working under such as arriving to assignments that don't exist, setting for meeting that have been ether canceled or relocated.

This is just the tip of the iceberg as I now find that the disorganizations skills of management, is affecting the entire unit. In an effort to make our rough roads smooth, we decided to get to together while the manager was on vacation.

Recognizing that we may be biting off more that we can chew, we decided to consult our boss' boss. We had him come down and discuss the ramifications of our decision. After bring up each individual issue he recognized and agreed that something must be done and that we were handling our situation properly, thus far. With a list of all our suggestions and things we would like to see changed, we anticipate some form of dispute you see more than half of the suggestions we are submitting to management involve changes taking place with him. How to change something that involves a human life. But then doesn't everything, I mean, involve a human life. When an employee has a problem with performance, who is the first person to tell them so. Sure, if a true friend exists and can see the on coming problem he can warn before the managerial train comes puffing down the track. But in most cases that train comes in full steam and executes his will on the cities he passes on his track to ego or self-gratification. Why should it be any different when it is that very locomotive who is told of there own problems. After all, if all the machinery operates in order, everybody gets where they want to go. So that's what this weeks Idea Journal is all about. When the plan is submitted at the next meeting, decisions are going to have to be made. All we know is that we are doing what we think is right the best way we know how. So is it fear that clenches me each time I think about the consequences? And what consequences, what can really be done to us? And probably the most interesting question of all, can the person who criticizes handle being criticized?

7-29-07 Driving just enough food to last until payday: The exact amount of TV dinners but plenty of beer and wine. Being in debt seems to be somewhat of a tennis match. A game against society and me. They served the ball the day I was born. I'm served a responsibility. Back and forth, up and down, I survive playing by the rules of someone else yet subconsciously recognizing that the most experienced player wins. I loose and win on daily bases, but at least I do have some control of the ball. I make the choice not to be arrested, the choice to educate myself to a better job and means to get there. I have the mind to think about the next play and how my opponent may try to defeat me. Sometimes I win, sometimes I loose but I often find that my loosing is because I'm not constantly watching out for the enemy.

7-31-07 DRIVING—I give up! Didn't I know what I was doing? How could I have done such a thing? Is there such a thing as preconceived wants? Explaining to my wife how difficult it is to do my homework assignment because of all the ruckus at the school lab. I determined that it might be better for me to do my homework assignments at home. To achieve this I would need to purchase a Mac computer. She (always so lovingly) agreed. We arrive at the Mac store with a stack of credit card receipts. I can't remember exactly where in the mall the store resides but we accidentally park near the front. "This must be God wanting me to buy this computer tonight". Now with God's approval I know I'm doing the right thing. We head straight for a sales person and begin an in death interrogation. After determining the computer requirements I make a mad dash to an empty stall and begin to calculate my unused credit. We calculated $2700 available credit. About $1000 short of this new computer we wanted. Or is it "I" wanted. We leave the store laughing and consider ourselves blessed.

8-1-07 Idea Journal—Can't take my eyes off of it. Finally completed the first scene in our film project my wife and I are working on. The EXT. A shot of her coming home one night while her best friend regurgitates her life's experiences on the phone to her. I know it's a little dark but I'm still proud of it. We should shoot the next scene in about two weeks. This is a very exciting camera test. We may even be able to use it in a film festival or at least for our own little screening with friends. It's called "In A Moment of Time", a story about a woman who get fired from an advertising agency. Her friends disagree with the boss and support her idea to start her own company. We soon experience first hand her gift of imagination and become totally engulfed in the way she gets back on her feet. "In A Moment of Time" look for it in at a theater near you.

8-2-07 Driving—Got an A—in Television Production on our first quiz. Midterm coming up next week gota study.

8-3-07 Driving—Talked to a friend about my financial situation. He says don't use the credit cards to get the computer. Get a job first to supplement the computer payments. Called my wife to talk to her friend who is the wedding coordinator at the church. "Tell her we will cut her a special deal" I say.

We will charge $1000 per camera and give her $200 per gig. Wife says her friend accepts the deal. We need to advertise so maybe I can find information on just exactly how to get this business up and running for our new computer.

Idea Journal—What to do! What to do! "In His Presence" the story of two girls who become the best of friends on a graveyard shift. Joyce is more mature than Kathy but Kathy more street wise. Their friendship explores a better way of life until Jason comes on the scene to bring back the past. A past filled with pain, anger and distrust from a world of internet pornography. Sooooo . . . What do ya think? Maybe 'In His Presence' would bring in money to get the computer. I figure about $4000 to produce the show. My friend said don't use the credit cards to purchase the computer but he didn't say I shouldn't produce a play. Maybe I should have told him about it, any way, I'll start smoothing out the script right away.

8-4-07 Idea Journal—"Why I Feel A Sense of Gratitude"? As you may recall, in our last episode, we touched on the very sensitive topic of "The Last Time I Cried". You may remember that while attempting to begin my tour of duty I was arrested by my very peers. This incident occurred over two years ago yet reared it's ugly head just last week. While being interviewed, regarding a totally unrelated incident, I was asked "If I myself have ever experienced anything I thought was unfair while working on the department". Mister, you picked the wrong person to ask that question to, (I thought to myself). I started from the very beginning. It was interesting to see how the expressions changed on the faces of my three on-lookers from across the table. I explained how I was surrounded by police officers and held at bay even though all of us were wearing the same uniform. Any motion picture screen would have been delighted to see such given attention. The gleam of their eyes at first read disbelief, but the quivering in my voice quickly subsided any doubt as I concluded with my disappointment of that night. Without hesitation, a Sergeant stood to his feet, held his hand out and with what I conceived to be the most sincere I'd ever heard, "On behalf of the Los Angeles Police Department, sir, please accept my apology to you for any discomfort or embarrassment we may have caused". An apology duly accepted. How little we know about the words we speak, how the person takes them we deliver them to. I believe success is defined by the choice of words we use. Without first considering the word we are about to give, we can eject an effect that will last a lifetime. Or through wisdom and common sense, we can stop to take a look around and question if that word we are about to deliver will lift a person up, or pull him down. An intangible weapon it is, that word we give. When shot from the barrel of one man can bring horror and pain yet when shot the barrel of another, helps to heal.

8-7-07 Idea Journal—A once in a life time scene. Yesterday while coming home I was on the 210 East. Noticing that the WB traffic had slowed I reasoned it to be because of the stalled vehicle located in the WB fast lane. Being in the EB Fast lane that gave me a nice view of what was about to take place. Just as I passed the stalled vehicle my eye was attracted to the sparks emitting from a 1950 Chevy being towed and obviously unbeknown to the driver had lost the front end was being drug across the freeway. With my venue now quickly becoming a lookie-lu lane the WB traffic came to a stop due to a woman who had run over something large enough to stop her car. She was getting out of her car to investigate from the center lane traffic, with all three vehicles in clear view, what a scene? A scene that I may never as long as I live see again, unless of course it were to be recreated in a movie. But then, maybe that's what this exercise is all about.

Driving—When you have someone that loves you enough to do whatever you say, you have to be cautious of your words. I clearly would never do anything to go against the grains of life but this was the second time sense our marriage that I felt it necessary for both of us to visit the Check into Cash facility. $600 we borrowed at 400%. That boils down to $490 received and $110 given away. For what ever reason in a few days the automatic payments are going to collide. Unless this money were deposited in the next day or so we would be paying $300 in bounce fees. I'm hoping that this is just the way the cards fell. I'm hoping that the next billing cycle will mean that we will have extra money. I'm hoping that I will be smart enough to leave that money alone and let it take care of it's self for the next flood of automatic payments. The news reports it everyday, that things are getting worse. Making enough money doesn't seem to matter. Two jobs don't seem to matter. A financial plan doesn't . . . well, it's got to be me.

But what have I bought? Food! Gas! That's it.
My plan is failing, next weeks payday is going
to be short $600 when we pay back the loan. Is
it true I have descended to living day by day.
Worse, convinced another human bean to dive
into the toilet with me. Am I the only one on
the planet who receives these letters from the
bank that state that they are raising their
prices for the service they offer.

I'm paying a bank to allow my money to set on
their computer. Something has got to change,
I think it's me but how?

8-10-07 Driving—So far so good, we are caught
up and on time for all bills until the next
pay day in a few days. I might add that the
automatic payment process does help to keep
your credit square. Even if you go overdrawn
the bank pays your creditor. Now I know this
is somewhat ridiculous but I'm starting to
look at loosing money to over draft fees as an
investment, a means of obtaining good credit.
I don't know if the bank reports your over
draft fees but I sure as heck know that if the
credit card company does not receive the money
on the agreed time that will surely go on your
record. Hey listen to this, I heard the other
day that credit card companies rely look at
the date they receive your payment. Something
about if you pay on time that means that you're
the average payer backer. So evidently there
are those who pay back their debt late, then
those who pay back on time and then those who
pay early. I heard that if you pay early that
rely looks good and is held in a most favorable
consideration. I have change all my due dates
to be paid automatically about a week before

they are actually due. Don't think this is
easy, you are constantly playing a game with
your pay check. I don't have a second job at
this time so I makes it a little more difficult
to hit this change in pay schedules but it's
kind of fun to try not to have to cancel the
automatic payments before they are sent out by
the bank.

Got a new credit card. Remember I told you
about that Mac computer we wanted for $5000
or whatever? Well the company I originally
applied for sent me a card worth $2200 so I
could buy the computer. So far I have put $50
on it for gas. This is intentional so I can
receive a bill. When the bill comes I will
pay it off and maintain a $20 per month going
into the account. Let me take a brake for a
moment and tell you what else I learned. If
the balance of what you charge can't be paid
off in three payments, you should not make
the purchase. That is my intention with this
new card but isn't that what I said about the
other cards which by the way equal $10,000.
But above all else, please take a moment to
think about this. How did I get this card?
You know what I mean. The bank just doesn't
start off by giving a new customer that much
of a limit, unless they think you are good for
it. Come on now, I know you may not want to
agree with this but it's called established
credit. Given, my established credit may only
be in plastic but I look back on my life and
clearly remember the day I which I could have
borrowed $100 for this or that. All this talk
about automatic payments, being on time and
paying early pays off. I still think the world
is cheating us. All the tricks and gimmicks

expose themselves everyday and we silly humans just complain and whimper but we refuse to gather together and take over the government so what's a hard working American to do?

Idea Journal—WOW! What a film! Much better than I imagined! Bourne Ultimatum, the hell with rules. How dare my film class attempt to express to me how important it is to follow the rules of camera angles and focus. All that went out the window in this one. The rules were so not adhered to, infant, I think I saw some camera angles that have never been done before. Zooms in and out, mostly hand held stuff, plenty Dutch tilts. I would think that for the editing, they went to the first day of editing school and picked out the most dependable student then said "here, have at it". The chops, cuts, sometimes freaky moves kept me in a state of shock but the most astonishing shot to me was well worth the waiting. The cameraman followed as the actor jumped off the top of a building and into the window of the building next door. I had seen the still of this shot in a magazine. It was the most impressive shot in the film.

8-12-07 Driving—I forgot to tell you this is the time of the year that I receive an extra check. That is to say that there will be no deductions taken out on the 31st, the entire amount is at my disposal. It may sound like a good thing and in a way it is. It's just that you have to be real careful and diligent in the way you think about all this extra money to spend. You see, by not having any deductions gives me about $700 extra. It must be used to do some good. The only good is to pay off a credit card bill starting wit the lowest balance. I know most experts say pay off the one with the highest interest but if I have one bill at 24% and a balance of $3000 and another bill at 16% with a balance of $295 and another a 14% with a balance of $195 and another at 12% with a balance $75 it just seems obvious to me to use the extra $700 to pay off the three bills that would eventually cost me much more in the end. In fact, the $700 would only apply money to the $3000 balance and still leave me with zero options to pay off the other cards accept to just wait and give away the interest fees. Eventually the cards would get paid off but I may have spent $3000 in principal and interest that just equals a whole lot of money gone to waste. So, in just two weeks away, lets see what I do.

Later—Sometimes those unexpected things get in the way. Got a letter in the mail from Capital One. They say my wife has a past debt of $1302.93. They are offering a settlement of $755.70. My first thought is to contact them and verify the debt; you know the scams goings on today one can't be too careful. After I confirm the situation I will consider alternatives to take advantage of the settlement. Isn't that interesting, $700 extra in two weeks and $700 in new bills. Is that how life is supposed to be? I thought it was love that makes the world go round.

Journal—"Why I Want Them to Know Me" Cranking half way through my first film class and I'm not quite sure of my thinking regarding getting what's on my mind into the minds of others. Information comes on daily bases to inspire

me to press on. Though I do recognize that
getting involved with school was the right
thing to do, I guess I'm just impatient. I
now find myself re-writing movies as I watch.
Sometimes I come up with what seems to be a
better scene or ending. I seem to find myself
more critical now that I'm in film school. I
focus in on things like lighting and audio and
enjoy the commentary more than the film itself.
This is somewhat of a welcome metamorphous for
me (To evolve from a spectator to judge and
jury). All my life I've seen films from only
one perspective then one day awakened to find
a whole new world. What else is there in life
to be awakened too? Heaven forbid that I pull
off a production and then realize that it's
just a process and not as impossible as I had
imagined. Shame on me to find that I didn't
have to wait until I obtained a million dollars
and completely out of debt before I could have
shot my own feature film. If it's one thing I've
learned, it's that I need people who believe
in me. People who I also respect, to start
something and hang in there to its completion.
I think I'm on the right track. I feel all of
these issues will come to light as I continue,
continue this transparency from one class,
one thought to another and recognize that I am
doing my films. Every time I learn something
new I go back to those scripts and re-vamp the
things that once prevented me from winning the
last film festival. Renewing my technique and
putting my dots and tittles in all the right
places. One day things will fall into place
then they will wonder where did this guy come
from? Is he the same one we once knew? The one
we once rejected who now becomes one of us.

8-15-07 Should be a financially interesting day. A settlement with Capital One for $660.00 will be taken out of my account to pay off an old Capital One account. A letter will be sent to confirm the paid in full and the credit report should reflect the same in a few months. I have arranged my checking account to pay off one of my wife's bills ever 15th of the month. We have an interview Friday with a new apartment complex. The monthly cost will save almost $400 in rent and gas. I figure that if we can't make extra cash on the side maybe we can get out of debt by lowering our existing spending obligations. This is a Senior apartment complex offering us $700 rent in stead of our present $950. It is 30 miles closer to work saving me about $150 a month in gas but my wife will be driving 20 miles more per day. The real savings is in the drive home. It is not unusual for me to take 3 hours to get home from L.A. Did I mention the new credit card? My wife, Cindy, and I needed a computer for editing in fact, a Macintosh with Final Cut Pro software, about $4000 worth of goodies including the software. I was approved for . . . wait a minute, seems like I told you this already. Never the less, I have used $300 on my credit card for schoolbooks and gas. Let's see what I do about paying it off.

Journal—thinking on today, school is top of the list. My dismay with going to school started on the last day I attended which was last Friday. After being given instructions to have my project digitized I was given the footage to work on. So I thought it was given to me. You see, one of the students digitized the footage and thought she was giving the footage to me. When I try to work with it I find that I have only the files, not the media, in other words it was of no use to me. A further attempt to contact the original owners of the footage failed as they were out of town with the master reel. Another attempt to contact the student with the digitized footage failed as she has yet to start working on her project. Two mistakes learned on this one. One—check and double check. I should have actually looked at my footage before I left class the day I thought it was given to me. Two—I should have digitized it my self if nothing more than to get the experience. Yet this incident I believe proves a point that I have believed for some time now. The more people you add to your projects in life, the greater your chance for Murphy's Law. As director, you have to pay attention to every detail and always try to work with competent people.

8-16-07 The Capital One Account did get paid off. Did you know there is a web site that will give you ratings regarding the apartment complex you live in? That place we were going to visit today, I just happened to look up what past and present residences had to say about it. It got a 12% out of a possible 100%. The comments are made public for all to see. The best comment stated something like. "You will just love it here, this is the perfect place for you—if you like walking around necked after being stripped by gang bangers looking for the next human sacrifice". That's to bad; we were sure looking forward to the savings. The wife wasn't mad at me; she said, "I guess you get what you pay for". We continue the saga searching for ways to save. By the way,

we also paid off the Check-into-cash account.
Never borrow money from those guys unless you
know for sure that you can pay them off in one
shot from your very next pay check you get and
only under the conditions that the interest
they charge is going to be less than any other
penalty you may be presented. In other words
do not use these payday loan companies except
to save you money. If you know that a check
you've written is going to bounce and the bank
is going to cost you $35 for the check fee and
going to the check cash place will only cost
you $25 then you save $10. The problem comes
when you get addicted to these places and
borrow until you become slave then you're in
trouble. Use only in emergency.

CHAPTER 21

LET'S GET BACK IN DEBT

8-18-07—Hang on to your wallet it's going to be a rough one. After explaining that we may have to hit Check-into-Cash for $300 initiated a question from my wife. She asks, "if we need money now to hold us over until the next payday, why are we tripling the minimum payments of out credit cards?" I explained that we are loosing money by only paying the minimum. Credit card companies have intentionally lowered there minimum payment due to extend the life of the loan, therefore extending your payments and the interest you pay thus increasing there profit. Are you noticing something? I'm noticing something, are you? People are making money off of you everywhere you go. The desire to get your money has broken race barriers. White sales people treat me better than black sales persons. I'm telling ya, this should tick you off knowing that, in everything you do someone is trying to figure out ways to take from you that which is rightfully yours. I double my credit card payments and when the payment is paid in full I continue paying $20 per month towards the account. I think I may have mentioned the effects of this action a few weeks ago. The thought of turning your credit card account into a savings account bewilders people. Try it sometime and watch what happens. When the credit card company owes you money, they quickly send it back to you in the form of a check.

Journal—A visit with family and friends and it's picture time. Everyone gathers in the living room while camera batteries warm up. It takes a while for all the women and girls to get into the perfect pose. The main camera begins the count down from 3 and just before the shutters clicks some jerk in the back of the room says STOP! All eyes turn to the intruder as silence yields a chance to explain the command. The jerk speaks up and this is what I explained. "The position you guys are in will cause your faces to be darken by the extremely bright background. Everyone quickly admitted they didn't consider the light until I said something. The moral of this story is that I am starting to use my film training in daily living situations. Everyone traded places and the pictures came out fine. Sometimes we're oblivious to reality until we receive an education in life.

8-25-07 Journal—Experiencing great rejection for some reason:

I think I'm being trained for something great. Not that I'm not use to rejection but I'm noticing the rejection bug crossing my path more than usual. Rejected from two auditions for movies but accepted to the cast and crew part for a previous project I worked on. Ideas rejected at work then proven they would have been successful, if considered. Rejected at the last minute to document a wedding only after all the equipment was collected and prepared. Daily rejection prepares me for tomorrow. After all, how else can I get use to my scripts being sent back to me and I produce them myself, and a blockbuster be born. I'll show em, reject me will ya! Bend over world cause I'm coming and I'm gonna kick ya where the sun don't shine. Remember the name.

Driving—Four days till payday. Gotta come up with a plan to take advantage of extra money. Gotta pay off stuff but things aren't looking good. I have a question for you. If I'm tripling my credit card payments, would it do any good to just pay the minimum for a few months and take the extra money added to the bills to pay the card down and accumulate it to pay off a bill? I need to do some calculations—be right back . . . Don't ever pay just the minimum. According to my credit repair resource, by paying just the minimum increases the balance. You will end up paying much more than to original cost of the merchandise by just paying the minimum. Soooo . . . my bright idea about cutting down the payments of my credit cards was justifiably stupid. I guess I should be proud of myself. Most people knowing that they were going to have extra cash heading there way worry about what they are going to buy for themselves. In some cases even writing checks to cover futuristic income, we call them faith checks in church. Here I am trying to figure out how to spend extra money on paying off a credit card or two. It should be interesting as always, just a few more days to go and I'll let you know what else I have gotten myself into.

8-30-07 I wish I were enthusiastic enough to go back and see what happened to the extra money I received 6 months ago. Is this some sort of pattern I have? I'm financially stupid I know but some things just don't add up. Well, as you know, I got an extra $1000 on my paycheck yesterday. The plan was to pay off a credit card or two. According to my calculations I should have been able to pay off three. But nooo, slick Steve scheduled automatic payments totaling an additional $1000. That's right my accounts broke me even. The wife paid back Check Into Cash and had just enough for the rent. I'm slowly watching my dream of paying off a card dwindle away. Don't ask me how I could not have foreseen this. All and all, not a single bill has been late in the past 6 months and I understand that's a good thing. The first payment to the new credit card (you remember, the one I was suppose to buy a computer with) was made in advance included in that $1000 money blunder I just made.

9-8-07 Driving—I have had three children from previous marriage and am currently married to my present wife Cynthia (Cindy).

$1000 must be the magic number because that's exactly what the mother of my first child wants per month for 170 months. It's child support season folks, that time of the year when people who suddenly feel that they did not get enough in the original order think they deserve some astronomical payoff for having, at sometime in your life, a marital association with you. Granted, I officially was ordered to pay $200 a month for 15 years ago, back in 1985. She only got the first year of the money including what she got from my retirement and any savings I had when I got the hell out of dodge. This new and improved adjustment stems from an association I managed through a marriage in 1982. Things got crazy and I left the State. My daughter is married now and mommy wants to be paid for wedding ceremonies endured. I did the calculations but have yet to figure out how $200 per month for 15 years comes out to be $170,000. Anyway, the letter from the attorney is addressed to the City Controller (the people who issue my pay check) advising the City of Los Angeles to send $500 every two weeks to the attorneys office starting on my next pay day. Now, this could be heart wrenching for some and even an opportunity replace your brain matter with lead for others, but please allow me to show you how to handle this situation. Let's start off with the worst-case scenario. Lets say for instance that in three days (on my next pay day) my paycheck is somewhat short, say like $500. That would be a clear indication that this attorney lady has a true love for runaway, lowdown deadbeat dads who are striving to learn from their mistakes and need to be shown that attorneys can supersede any judges ruling and come up with absolutely any figure a vivid imagination will grant. It would be the end of attempting to continue this book because there would be no way I could ever get out of debt paying that outrageous amount. It could affect ones marriage, causing one to think that there is no way to be happy so why pull someone else down the toilet with me. At least save one soul by getting a divorce. Why should my current wife who had absolutely nothing to do with the situation have to pay for my mistakes? Well here's the deal. My wife loves me and understands that I have a past. She also must be aware that I'm not the person that I was 30 years ago. She is willing to stick with me thick and thin and that is going to take a lot of glue. If I pay for the crime I must do the time. Upon noticing a shortage in my check we thank God for the ability to make ends meet and get an attorney of our own and deal with the situation. Isn't it funny how people suddenly get religious when they are in trouble? Anyway, everything happens for a reason. Your very existence is specifically timed. You thought you came up with that idea by accident, no way. If the money doesn't come out of my check this would be even sadder. It would mean that there are people out there who would bring themselves down to the ground level by lying, deceiving and attempting to cheat you without even establishing some form of communication to try to work things out. It would leave me with an impression about attorneys. It would show me that for a few dollars, they would be willing to use a good education to be become criminals themselves. It would mean that the documents I received regarding the $1000 monthly payments were forged. Forged to look like they came from the court. Excuse me, but don't we hire attorneys to protect us from people like that. Nevertheless, in three days I will know if this book suddenly comes to an end. Don't worry about reading through to the last page. Thumb through quickly—right now to see if there are more pages. It could be a trick; the rest of these pages are blank just to deceive you.

9-16-07 Unexpected money missing from my account. This is terrible, how could this happen to me? Four bounced checks; AAA Auto started taking money out for my premium this month. Yeah sure they sent me a letter stating that it was going to start but they didn't have to follow through. That forgotten withdrawal cost me $150 in service charges with B of A. But I'm not mad; better $150 than $170,000. That's right, maybe evil lurks around the corner of the next paycheck but for now I have been given grace. This is not a time to rejoice, you see, I totally understand the laws of life. "What goes around comes around" so let me just shut my mouth and live on. Gas prices are crazy; I'm spending $500 per month just on gas. I decided to solve the problem by looking for a motorcycle. I drove around but couldn't find a dealer. My wife said, "I agree with saving gas and a motor cycle may help us out". I explained to her that we could go to the mountains camping on it. She said, "That would be fun". I told her we could go to Las Vegas and cruise down the strip. She said, "I would like to learn how to drive it". I told her all the goodies you can get with your motorcycle that make life more comfortable if she just let by buy one. She said; "I trust you in handling our financial situation, do whatever you think is right". I quit looking for a motorcycle. The $200 hundred dollar per month gas savings do not cover the $200 per month payment, $33 per mo. for insurance, $5 per mo. maintenance, $10 per mo. extended warrantee and so forth. Nice to have a wife who agrees but getting out of debt takes wisdom.

It's off to Las Vegas, a friend hired us to film a gospel concert. Chalk another $300 to Fountain of Life Productions. It's the end of the first quarter at school and my business takes a turn for the better.

9-17-07 All is well on the money side things going as planned. That is, automatic deductions are being made and a comfortable reserve is in the account. Sometimes I just think I'm spinning my wheels. $300 I just deposited will be gone in a few months. Not because of spending it but in service fees from bounced checks I mentioned earlier. Those of you who are rich would already know how to increase the money so it pays it's own service fees. You probably work at the bank where I made the deposit. Well until I figure it out; don't spend all the interest I just paid you all in one place.

9-22-07 Yesterday was the last day of school for the quarter. I guess an "A" is not bad but that was only one class. Lets see what happens next quarter with three classes to tackle. The reason I bring up school and compress it within a book about how to get out of debt is because of something that happened to me the other day. If your considering education while getting out of debt school will definitely put a crunch on you dream plans. In going to school I was able to obtain a $30,000 loan. I had only used $27,000 by the end of the quarter. The financial department called me in to advise me that I had such a credit and what did I want done with the money. I could have a check cut or have it sent back to the people who so kindly gave me the money. This is not a good thing. I find out later that the actual amount of the loan was actually $10,000. The other $20,000 was finance charges. This loan is to be paid back at $170 per month for so and so amount of years and begins 6 months after I graduate. And that's just for this first year;

I have two more years to go. I understand that my entire education processing will cost me in the realm of $80,000 for film school. This will be a BS degree in film. Anyways—what I wanted to get to is the fact that this overpayment will happen every quarter. Now there is the problem my friend. You see at the rate I'm going, I figure that since it's a loan anyway and it's my money, why not use the money every quarter towards getting out of debt. Now before you graduates start screaming, no! In slow motion, tell me if I'm wrong. My current credit cards charge anywhere from 14% to 28% right? It just seems right to pay off the cards that have a lower interest rate than the payoff amount of my loan. Okay! I'll take your screaming into consideration and rethink the situation. Tell ya what; I'll get some financial counseling from the financial department when they call me in to pick up the check.

9-24-07—At least they gave me warning that my credit card limit was approaching. $1.00 over the limit, that's what they say but how can that be? I haven't used that credit card in three months. In fact—not since I bought my wife that hair kit that saves us money by not going to the hairdresser. When I purchased the hair care kit I agreed that they could take out $39 a month for three months. Wait a minute, we save $30 on the hairdresser and spend $35 in over the limit fee. What a society we live in, you would have to pay somebody to keep ahead of the financial game but I'm learning a very important lesson. It seems the things that catch me off guard and almost always cost me extra money are the things that happen automatically. Some companies agree to take out monthly payments on your approval and you just forget that it's that time of the month. If at all possible, avoid any automatic deductions from companies that don't send you monthly statements. Unless of course you are astute enough to write it down on the calendar or put a piece of paper with the companies name and with drawl date in with your monthly bills to remind you. I keep my monthly bills categorized individually according to the name. The main thing is you want to be able to easily compare last months bill with the current one—each month. This helped me catch a mistake on my statement last week. A statement with a payment due on the 31st showed a late fee of $29. My records showed that my automatic payment went in on the 31st therefore the accounting was done on the same day, as the payment was due. I called the company and they confirmed that the payment was indeed received on the 31st and adjusted my account accordingly. It seems that companies are picking up speed in mistakes that seemingly tend to lean in their favor if you don't catch it.

9-27-07 Word is that interest on school loans are going to go down. One year and six months to go before my retirement will be paid off. I can't tell you what page it's on but I did mention that I was in the process of executing a retirement buy back.

That is, purchasing previous time worked for another employer. I understand that if you can deal with the deductions until paid off it is a well worth investment in your future. I plan on retiring soon there after. Did I also mention not retiring in California? My little retirement would go much further in another state.

Yesterday's payday went smoothly. The wife deposited what would normally be used as the rent into my account. I'm using my money to pay the rent and hers is used to get her out of debt. My plan is that around the first of the month we will give ourselves a loan. Remember the money we made filming the gospel concert? That $400 would be used to help make the rent payment then put back after the next paycheck. It sure beats the interest at check-into-cash. But lets see what really happens.

10-8-07 What really happened was nothing life at all. The $400 did not get replaced. It was used to play catch up and or left in the account as a cushion to prevent overdrafts. I can't recall if any plan of mine has worked since I started this stupid book.

A bit of good news! The wife and I were called to shoot a wedding. $350 was collected the day of the filming and another $350 will be due at the time the edited master is delivered. A bit of bad news we both visited Check-into-Cash this week. Please don't ask, I don't know what happened. We bought nothing, absolutely nothing that would intrude on our plans. The only thing I can say is to wait until the next pay cycle in about a week. Hopefully we see extra cash to be left in the bank for the following cycle. Another cycle seems to be lingering in the background. All the bills are becoming due at the same time. To notice this means that we are keeping up with our money and watching the accounts closely, and I thank God for an understanding wife. It also means a change up in having extra money for fun for a while. Did I tell you about the school contacting me to inform me that I didn't use up the allotted student loan money? I may have also said how important it is <u>not</u> to accept the check due to high interest from the loaning banks. I picked up the $2700 check I stated not to accept on the 10th. The plan is to pay off $2500 worth of credit card debt. Lets see what I do next.

The wife and I are very serious about the music we write and believe that offering our music to the public would be advantageous to us financially. What has held us back for so long is the fact that the equipment needed to produce our material was not in our budget. It is just too much to spend on an unsure thing. Yesterday while making our customary dream visit to the music store, we were convinced that we could make our current equipment work for us with just two additional pieces of equipment, a mixer and software. We made the purchase, $1000 was approved on credit not due for 12 months. Oh, you know me by now, the debt will be paid off before the year is up but we figured that we are worth the investment. Only time will tell the fate of our new direction on the road to driving myself out of debt via the release of our first CD.

10-10-07 The simple explanation comes from my wife. I explained my dilemma as to not understanding why we suddenly needed more money and that I had deposited an extra $800 in our account including the Check-into-Cash loan. My attempt to explain to her that we should be okay until next week on payday was interrupted; my wife replied "What do you mean next week, payday is today".

In my astute desire to avoid not having enough money to cover the incoming automatic deposits, I miscalculated our paydays. To make a long story short, we are $800 in the black. By the way I did get the check from my school loan today and did deposit it in the bank. $2780 plus the normal $800 my wife usually transfers plus the $800 over deposit that I made. This should be a very interesting session on the next reading.

10-14-07 5 count 'em 5 credit cards paid in full, Check-Into-Cash paid off and any bills with a balance of $300 or less was paid in full. It is very rare indeed that you have such an opportunity to hit your debts with such small sums of money but now is not the time to let your guard down. Money-grubbing situations tend to have a keen sense of smell when you're getting a-head in life and pop up when you least expect it. With $2000 remaining in savings it's time to watch. Keep looking around to see which direction the unexpected money-grubbing enemy will strike next.

For once in a few moons you have the upper hand, but remember, the enemy of debt is not fleeing he has only taken cover and waiting for his next opportunity. Don't advance, don't retreat, hold your ground. All this caution is making me hungry. We're meeting some friends in Old Town Pasadena for lunch. Gonna talk about our little video company and pick up the tab. Don't worry, every soldier dips into his care package every now and then, and we deserve it!

10-15-07 A call from Sam's Club causes me to think they are in on the deception game. They say that I am late with my payment and that the current balance of $239 includes the $30 dollar late fee. My wife is updating our financial database as the call comes in. "Honey, would you please take a look at the last Sam's Club statement and tell me when it was received". "Two months ago" she replies. Beware of creditors that do not send your statements regularly. You must review your payments regularly so you send a payment even if you don't get a statement. The debt monster appears in the form of a late fee. If I'm not mistaken those jokers did this to me once before but who's fault is it that the bill wasn't paid? That's why I'm not complaining. The debt monster snaps at you even when he is on the ground. This is so ridiculous; wait until after you are late to tell you, you are late. You can't tell me that they didn't know that I was going to be late. There is probably some poor so and so just pulling due dates making sure that no contact is made until after you owe a late charge then they call you to thank you for the generous donation. Anyway—like I said it's my fault. I shouldn't depend on a statement to tell me when my payment is due. I'm watching my account very closely. The plan is to watch and see what happens for the next three weeks when my wife's check comes in and see if we're able to pay off anything. By the way, I received a call from her a few hours ago. She said that the breaks are squeaking.

Do you smell the cost of a break job coming up?

10-19-07 The debt monster dies slowly. The results begin to trickle in; negative balances on credit card accounts now say the bank owes me money. A tag team is established. My wife checks behind me making sure that I have fired accurately at the monster but we both know he is still lurking below. As long as blood pumps through his vines there is a chance he could still strike.

You've seen those movies where the approaching creature get hits by a chair and knocked out? You don't just walk away from those guys; they always get up and grab you from behind. You have to cut off their head while they're unconscious then you can live another day but nooooooo! We want to have sequels in life and call it adventure when the debt monster recuperates. Stop and watch, don't do anything just watch as the first assault takes effect. Leaving $1000 in the account as a cushion gives me more ammunition incase of a surprise attack. Somehow I think that disciplining yourself with a budget and trying to constantly be aware of your spending helps you not to yield to temptation when a large sum of money comes your way. Yes we went crazy with our friends last week spending $100 on dinner but it would have been so easy to take the money from the school loan and buy some things that we have been wanting. The key thinking here is that the $2700 check from school was not a gift. I did not find it in a bag somewhere, in other words, it must still be paid back to the bank or who ever gave me the student loan. No sense in rejoicing over the amount of money now available to spend when in actuality, the moment you spend someone else's dollar, you have to pay them back three. I'm still convinced that there are only two logical uses for a credit card, and in both cases in which you are not the recipient of the increase. If you are the bank you have plenty reason for someone to owe you money because there are plenty someone's willing to pay the interest. But for the experienced monster hunter, the only reason to have a credit card is first to establish credit, help pave the way to financial worthiness so those with the financial means may assist you in your financial endeavourers until you become the person those someone's come to for a loan.

The second reason is to have an instrument in your pocket to use as revenue rather than cash. To take advantage of opportunities that will save you money in the long run. But your main objective is to have that opportunity money in the credit card account prior to spending. What! Let me make myself perfectly clear. I have said it time and time again; use your credit card as a savings account. That way the money you charge is your own not the banks. Yes you may have to borrow from the bank by charging something but at least, worse case scenario, you will be in the habit of paying off the account within thirty days. Let me harp on this thirty days rule. If you can't pay off what you charge before the time the statement due date rears it's ugly head, you can't afford to charge it. May I go off track here for a moment? Sometime ago I mentioned that I was doubling up on my car payment. To

be exact, a 2007 Chrysler Town and Country
with a monthly payment of $300. It's a year
old now but since day one I have been paying
$600 per month. In the process of backing me
up, my wife checked the payoff just for the
records. The car payment requested for this
month is around $100. Can you get to that?
The financial institute only wants me to send
them $100 as my monthly payment. I can't wait
to see what happens next. Will the payment
drop down to a negative number? In other words
will the payment due eventually be—$100? In
that case they will start sending me the car
payment. Anyway, the loan company gets $600
automatically and that's that.

Let me also stick a pin in your back up plan. It
is so reassuring to have someone who believes
in what you are trying to do. I believe that
your partner can make or break you and I have
a real winner in the passenger seat while on
the bumpy road to financial success driving us
out of debt.

10-15-07 A representative from Sam's Club
calls to say that they have not received my
September payment yet. My wife happens to be
at the computer to check the account; and no
statement for September was received. Seems to
me this has happened before with this account.
I ask the man on the phone what the balance
is and send the entire amount via electronic
mail.

10-22-07 What did I tell you about the monster
never giving up. I receive a phone call from
Sam's Club. The lady on the phone says that
they have not received my September payment of

$15 and that a late charge has been added to my balance. I explain that a man called a few days ago and I paid off the account at that time. I gave her the information from my bank proving payment and she was very nice to take note of that fact.

This is first time, in quite a few months that I haven't touched my savings. I usually have to extract two hundred dollars automatically deposited on payday and apply it to an account just to make ends meet. I know that I will but it's just nice to know that things are changing for the better.

11-1-07 A three way conversation with Sam's Club, Bank of America and myself. It is determined that the payment I sent went to the wrong place. All is well for now and a zero balance incurs. Four more credit cards to go totaling $3500.

Joining the union with the LAPD was not such a bad idea after all. I received a check for $800 for tool allowance. The last $300 credit card has been paid off and I now move into paying off all cards with $400 maximum range. That execution should take place next week. Incase your interested; the four credit cards left to pay off are arranged like this. One for $460, one for $517, one for $800, the new credit card at the music store for $1000, and one for $1600. There are a few other installment payments like Home Depot and the like but my focus is on the people who don't have a lot of concern about my wellbeing. At least at Home Depot I can build a house to live in. Incase your still interested; the only vehicles to pay off is one van for $9000 and one van for $24,000. The bills after that are for monthly expenses that do not accumulate interest such as storage rent insurances etc.

10-13-07 Sometimes we welcome the debt monster with open arms even willingly bowing to circum to a critical attack. $3000, that's what it cost for the new iMac computer including editing software, speakers and a printer. It would be wisdom to stop and examine myself to see why I intentionally decided to fail my financial plan but I find no reason. I'm hoping this thinking justifies the reason I broke my own rules. There are actually people waiting for us to complete editing projects but the debt monster just kept introducing the need for more equipment. An interface here more powerful speakers there and before I knew it . . . but listen to this, in one week I realized that I had available to me over $5,000 in new credit. Two gas cards approved for $1000, Best Buy approved for $4000, continued letters advising of credit increases.

What a fool, the monster I was watching lying there, bleeding on the ground was a decoy. The real problem was occurring on the out skirts of town. In an attempt to get out of debt I was giving ammunition to other demons working on my credit rating, which attracted a larger crowd of demons. There are no excuses in warfare you can go down by several ways, friendly fire, and surprise attack or even be defeated on a routine mission. But to willingly step out into the open as I have is nothing less than suicide. Therefore I come to you with great adoration. I have failed, first myself and the egotistical stature I attempted to portray and my foolish thinking that someone like myself could change a system predestined to control you enough to willing submit. It's a drug, that's what it is a drug. Debt is a drug, addicting in every way and more detrimental to your health than most medically acclaimed deceases. With that I bid you farewell. Without accomplishment of my goal what good is continuing, these words just become some one's diary, a stinking journal keeping track of failure and defeat. Making public my humility and shame. So this book ends with submission and apology. I'm so sorry I thought myself so lofty to take up another human beings time in life to pay attention to a fool. Some of us teach as a fool, some preach and some are too foolish to recognize the fool but I have become the very person to watch out for. There are no words to ever replace the pain I've caused neither myself, nor the time I have stolen from you. So ends my story as I publicly admit that there is absolutely no way out of debt, no way to evade the monster and his cohorts so SPEND, SPEND, SPEND and live like everybody else. Signed Author of this stupid book—Steve Sloan.

10-14-07 To further conclude this final chapter, I receive a phone call today from the City Controller. She says that the child support judgment is in the hands of the City Attorney. She stated that because of the unusually large amount of back child support requested, the city attorney must make a decision as to how to proceed. What an opportunity to set things straight? I'm learning that opportunities get more expensive the more you wait. If I had taken care of business at the time of the

original court order not only would I have
saved $100,000 but also it would have been
paid off almost seven years ago. Let this
be a lesson ladies and gentlemen. If you owe
child support please pay it as the original
court order shut the hell up and live your
life. Is this an indication that if I don't
start paying now, that I could possibly owe
$100,000,000? That is if I live to be 65? The
important factor here is attitude. Let life be
a game. Everyday look for someone or something
to crush you, take away your joy. Once you are
conscious of the monster and his position of
attack, look him in the eyes and walk around.
That is true victory, and if you have someone
who loves you. Don't let your daily warfare
take a bite out of their life. They didn't
start your fight. They are there to back you,
help you with your armor when you get home from
battle. Trying to slay the beast in anger,
retaliation and vengeance only pisses him off
and you have much more to live for.

I watched the news the other day and saw a
doctor who got sued for millions of dollars
for mal practice. I saw a man gunned down in
the streets of L.A. only half my age. With
just those two observations, someone is being
forced to give more money than I am and younger
people than me are not breathing anymore. Those
dreams and visions you have about success in
life. Look at those things not the things that
could cause you to veer off the road.

Yes we loose, but don't stop loving, yes
people take from more than they should but
that doesn't give you the right to take back.
Being angry at the world makes you part of it.

Keep smiling, don't tell everyone the trouble you're in, in fact, play the game of making people think you never have any trouble. You may have to make major joy adjustments but don't stop proceeding with your plans to retire at an early age, don't stop your aspirations of getting out of debt, it just may take a lot longer than you thought. So what! If you die tomorrow you died trying to get out of debt and if you don't die tomorrow the debt is still there so suck it up!

I'm currently looking for a way to supercharge this new way of thinking. I find myself failing quite often by thinking on the negative aspects of life. I have to stop myself and say, "Stop it, this is really happening to you, deal with it and move on". This is not easy when things are getting to you. When you're sitting there looking through your glass living room sweating from the heat mad at the guy who wrote a book that put you in that situation, it doesn't make it any easier. I guess the only excuse you should ever have not to do the things that make you happy is when you can't smile anymore, at least, not of your own free will.

12/14/07—I'm not back to stay, I'm ending this silly book. I just thought that you might like to know that I've changed the name of the book to "Parking Yourself Into Debt". This book is about how to be like everyone else. Crazy, debt riddled and down right mad at the world. First please allow me to appease you by telling you how much more debt I've gotten myself and my innocent loving wife into. I get this bright idea to make millions of dollars by editing videos. Went out and bought a new computer with all the gizmos. Feels good to be normal doesn't it, spend, spend, and spend. Recognizing that I needed a videotape machine that would play my digital tapes I went searching on E-bay. Need I say more? I found the perfect machine and got the owner down from $1400 to $1200 plus $44 shipping. The order was place about two weeks ago, since then I've lost time, money, time with my wife and friends, and . . . Well why don't I just let you read what has happened thus far.

On yesterday 12/13, I receive the machine, but it is not working, sent machine back at the cost of $65.00, and checked my e-mail to see if package arrived to sender. It got there this morning but strangely enough, the sender did not advise me that they received it. This could only mean one thing. That machine is now sitting on the counter, and the sender has my money and the returned machine. This, I might add is so embarrassing for a man who convinced his wife to make such an investment. My guess is that they are trying to fix the old machine I sent back instead of sending me another machine. One thing for sure—they found out that it was broken or they surely would have contacted me by now to tell me that I'm stupid and just didn't have the right button pressed. Anyway, I'm getting ready to check my e-mail and if I haven't heard from them I'm going to ask them what's up with the machine and send me another one now. To be continued . . .

In the meantime, the car is not running right, took it to my dependable mechanic, and $250 for a major tune-up. That did not solve the problem; mechanic is playing by the rules get all you can for doing nothing. I love it! Take the car to the dealer, they find the problem. $800 not including the rental car I had to get just to get home. My mechanic needs to take note, the more thieves you have working in one place, and the more you can steal.

All credit cards just about maxed out. Did you figure out by my entry dates that it's almost Christmas. Gonna go buy my wife some stuff—the Macy's account was in the plus—they owed me money. Told the wife "have at it baby, you know the rules around here—spend, spend, spend". I told her that the new name for the book is 'When you think you're out of debt, you're not so spend like hell'.

Today is the last day of school for this quarter, and we get three weeks off. I'm taking my wife to Universal Studios, gonna take her to lunch at Tony's and buy some real food then go get the car out of the shop. Hope you're enjoying this new form of thinking as much as I am. I just got a brainstorm how to use more of the little money I have. How about a song "Get All You Can" or "Anyway You Can Get It" or "To Hell With Other Human Beings" "Do Unto Others While They Are Doing You" or "Spend, Spend, Spend".

12/28/07—Don't mean to bother your spending but I just thought that since we are on the same track about being homeless; broke and mad is the only way to go—I spent $4000 for Christmas. Hee-ha! It feels good. $3400 of it was a debt that magically appeared from an old credit card account back in 2001. The original amount was $7000 but I settled with them. Charged the full amount to three credit cards. Now that I think about it, I can't think of a reason why I didn't just pay the $7000 Oh well! The other $700 was spent on things for the wife and I and a few friends and family but mostly on us. I didn't get any of the jobs that I interviewed for you know the white boys only jobs I applied for but there is a rumor that my position will receive retro pay and a 2% cost of living in the next few pay checks.

The apartment managers gave us $500 off the rent next month for renewing our lease I'm going to let the wife have it so she can stay in the habit of spending. She says it's okay for me to spend, spend, and spend on some new equipment to get our CD project out. For some reason she seems to think that if other people have opportunity to hear our music we will go back to the silly thought of being out of debt. Some people never give up!

12/28/07—First time viewers of their wedding will arrive tonight to see their final edit. The final payment of $350 will be paid if they like what they see. Buying all the equipment is beginning to pay off but a little late. With my new objective to spend—it matters not.

1/1/08—Happy New Year everybody! $800 extra in bank, thanks to the yearly union members tool allowance, but let's see how to spend it. $100 went to my wife last night in a banded stack of $1.00 increments as a gift on New Years. I'm sure I can find a way to spend, spend, and spend the rest. Maybe even on something that will get us even deeper into debt. But first—what takes you from this level? What keeps you from being in the same place year after year? How do you prioritize life to peek out at the most advantageous position possible? What a place to start figuring all this out—on the first day of the year. With all the talent instilled within, which one would best produce the most desired results? I turn to God in prayer for this one but something has got to be done.

3/27/08—I'm not continuing the book—I just wanted to make a little note for myself. Borrowed $10,000 from the credit union. Paid all credit cards accept one. Brought down interest rate from 21% to 8%. I figure by paying off the 9 credit cards I saved $1000 in interest and other ho humm stuff. The final credit card is $4000. Remember! I haven't stopped making the payments to each credit card I just paid them off and changed my monthly payment to them from the requested amount to $20 per month each.

CHAPTER 22

THE UPPER HAND

Seeing some weird stuff happening. My wife and I want to go to a seminar in Las Vegas. When I checked to see which credit card had the lowest balance, it was the card that had a $300 credit on it. In other words, the trip to Vegas up to $300 is absolutely free. Pre-paid if you will. I find that true more and more as I need money and go to see which credit card has got the most balance available with free money. I'm also receiving checks from the companies that just can't seem to stand me having a reserve in my account. They send me checks so my account is zeroed out. One thing that bothers me. One of my goals was to obtain an American Express Card. Do you know those fools rejected me. They say they based their decision mostly on the fact that I had to many inquires. Daaaa! How am I going to obtain good credit unless I ask for credit? I'll give it a year and try it again. Time to work on the wife's credit. Up till now everything has been in both our names. Should something happen to me; she needs to be able to get money on her own. I had her apply for money from my credit union. I'll put the money in savings and pay off the loan in 6 months then borrow more and do the same thing. I know she wants a house but the market is very scary.

People are loosing right and left. Some say that now is the time to buy, so many empty houses on the market, so, many scammers too.

I'll have to pray on this one. By the way, I did a gig last month, retirement party; $300 in the business account. Seriously looking at retiring in May of next year. Things are really touch and go for now, we still want to do the RV thing. Gotta pray on this one too. Did I tell you never to by a Chrysler. That's a big no no, no resale value. Next step is to pay the Chrysler down enough to be financed by the Credit Union. That would be about $7000 so we can get a lower interest rate. In fact the goal is to get everything financed at the lower rate then have only one payment going to the Credit Union.

Finally, concentrating on paying all bills off before retiring. I think we can do it! After retirement, I will only be making half of my current income. The plan is to make up the difference doing video and stage productions. It feels kind of different thinking about doing fun stuff for the rest of your life. My wife will retire about two years after me. This is a safety net just in case I forget to pray. Just a note to myself!

5/30/08 amazing how you can adjust to a life style forced upon you. I don't have to think too hard on how easy it was to get use to living out of my car. The yearning to create music, recording in the back seat, oh yes we adjust to things if given enough time. I have heard that some homeless people get use to living on the streets, so much so that they loose the incentive to change for the better. I'm so blessed to have Cindy in my life. She totally understands my reasoning.

The credit union has approved Cindy's loan for $3000 when she turns in her last check stub and verification of employment. Her prior credit report had showed three discrepancies. I paid off two and sent a letter to another until they were history. It took about three months to complete the process including ordering credit reports from www.annualcreditreport. com. She should be able to get money on her signature anytime she needs it. My plan is to take the three thousand dollars and put it into the same account the credit union takes the payments out of. Pay the debt off in six months then have her repeat the process until she can get ten thousand dollars on her signature alone. We will loose the cost of finance charge and interest but in the long run it's important for her to be able to get money when she needs it. Let me also mention a sense of comfort in her life knowing that there are no financial burdens in the way. Believe it or not, I believe that your sexual relationship can improve when your wife has no financial worries.

Did I tell you I received an offer for $4000 from HSBC at 0% financing for the first six months. I took it, paid off four credit cards with high interest and just made the second payment of eight hundred dollars yesterday. I simply divided the $4000 by six months and send in about $800 per month. They only require me to pay $45 per month but you know how to deal with that by now. I wrote on my calendar how much child support I owe. I've made three payments and am down to owing $169,000. My first child support I have been paying for my youngest child, will be paid off in June of this year. I checked with the agency just to get a rough idea of how much longer I could donate to my sons support. They say that three months prior to the child's 18th birthday, my ex-wife will receive a letter indicating that in three months the support will cease unless she can prove that the child is still in high school. If she cannot prove that he is still in school the support ends in April. At the end of this process this will give me an additional $475 income per month. Almost one half of the new child support payments per month, recent ordered for my oldest child. In February of next year I will be 55 and eligible for full retirement. In May of next year my buy back loan with the city will be paid off towards my retirement. This will add $500 per month to the income. It is estimated that when I retire next year that I will take home about $1500 per month. This calculation is excluding the $1000 per month for the new child support. Cindy and I both agree that we can get our production company up and running to offset the losses. Last year we made almost $2000 working Fountain of Life Productions part time. This year alone we have already surpassed that. I figure that the child support payment is God's way of pushing us into doing what He's called us to do. Christian entertainment, yelp—that's what I'm here for.

7/1/08—The attorneys say, "forget it". I only asked if there was anyway to lower the payments. "It's the 10% interest incurred over 25 years of sin. Well he didn't say sin but that's what it was. Not taking care of business when I was suppose to. If I would have paid the $200 per month like the court said to, I would not be looking at pay checks less $500 every two weeks. I have to get it through my head. It's my fault, I did it, I was wrong, I did not handle the situation right and I'm the only one to blame.

I talked to a realtor over the weekend. She said chances of getting a loan for a house are slim because of debt. Can you get to that! She didn't even mention how different we were not to have credit card debt. For me the spot light was on the car payment and child support that I pay. Look lady, if you're reading this book. Your so stuck on trying to make money in these hard times that you didn't even think to give someone credit for what you've read already. So we can't get a house right now, yeah you figured it right, I'll be 70 years old when my child support is paid off, but I have done some things in the past few years that you probably only dream of doing. I can't really say I was never alone. I always had favor with God so take your house and shove it.

Cindy and I continue to establish credit. We needed to sit on real chairs so we got a good deal at a furniture store for two recliners. They say no payment for one year but they got the first payment last week. I had Cindy take out a personal signature loan with the LAPD Credit Union. We asked for $10,000 just to see what would happen. They approved $3000 if she paid off two negative accounts on her credit report. They asked for $104 per month and got their first payment of $500 two weeks ago. I don't know but I get the impression that when a man handles all the finances in the family, then dies, the wife has a hard time dealing with everything, so at least consider her now, reestablish her so she can get money. If I have nothing else to offer, let me give to her life after my death.

You guys have been great! I'm sorry you had to put up with my ups and downs of confusion, lies and deception. I'm gonna read this thing from start to finish and see if I can give myself any tips on how to handle the rest of my life as I'm transported from place to place in a vehicle I really don't want to be associated with. While driving myself out of debt, so long everyone. Remember—being in debt is your faithful pet.

7/2/08—Yesterday I got the urge to stop by a Century 21 office to check on the purchase of commercial property. I'm thinking we need a theater of our own. The little Spanish man behind the counter was the first person who didn't laugh on the inside at the idea of our wanting to build a theater with no money in pocket. After a brief explanation he very politely got up and asked me to follow him to the back. Warming up his old computer I witnessed him take pot shots at the desktop targets with his rickety old mouse pointer that rarely hit the spot. Not being foolish enough to continue my dream discussion about how Cindy and I plan to use the property, I remained silent in hopes that it would expedite his attempt to show me his shooting gallery intention. Suddenly—bulls eye. The very dimensions I described popped up on his little screen. The cost of the facilities seemed to slap me in the face. But all within reach if only I had not made such terrible financial mistakes in life. That little man gave me hope "I know you can do it" he said. "Just continue to pay off bills, save half a million dollars then get back to me. Meanwhile, I'll keep an eye out for you". These are the hardest times any generation has ever experienced. Recession is misspelled by the denial of our current president. The man running to take his place spells depression out right. The world is changing quickly as we witness some races lower their weapons and decide to fight together. But is it to late? Bodies wash ashore into the nearest strip mall. Martin Luther King's dream is now a reality but at the cost of his own life. We still have such a long way to go. Looking for work, watching our backs, living—learning, testing the time to see if it's the right one for now. If it's one thing I've learned during these pages, it's that life is distracting. You desire to do one thing and fate shows you reality. The fate of the road each of us travels as we continue to accelerate to the next financial parking lot. Through all its curves and dead ends, we make more U-turns than any—while driving ourselves out of debt.

7/25/08—Paid off a credit union loan yesterday. It was only $600 but I'd had it for 7 years. It has a 10% interest rate. So whenever I had the chance I used it instead of any other credit card. I applied for another credit card. Stop calling me stupid and listen. The business—Fountain of Life Productions, needs a building. I need to establish credit for the name of the business. I received a notice that Capital One is sending a business card good for $5000. I have to start all over again. I now have to teach the company how to "drive its self into debt". May I have a side bar with you for a moment? Things are bad at this time. Marvin Gaye's song "What's Going On" was prophesied for today. As I write this portion I look down on several rolls of film that I'm about to transfer onto DVD. I mean reel film, 8mm super 8mm and 16mm film. I just completed editing a four-day shoot of a family reunion and was asked in the same week to operate a steadicam (a camera mounted to my body) for a musical. What I'm trying to say is that God is keeping us, my wife and I, and we don't necessarily see the effects of the child support or the recession. I guess I'm just trying to reiterate something I may have stated in the beginning of this book. The success in the process of driving yourself out of debt is credited for the most part on having a relationship with the highest God. It's that time again; the next paycheck I receive will not have any deductions on it. What will I do?

CHAPTER 23

DON'T DO AS I DO

7/26/08—Something stupid, I spent, spent, spent. You thought I was going to be smart didn't you? Get this—A credit card was approved for $5000 at 0% interest for 15 months. It's the first credit card for the Fountain of Life Productions Business. This is so cool; I've been trying for the past year to establish credit. There stipulation is that the card be used for business purposes only so I spent $1000 for office supplies. I can't wait to use the driving system to pay them off. My thinking is that this is the way to establish credit for the company in order to buy a building. At this date and time life is really bad. The Governor slashed 200,000 state employees down to minimum wage so to meet the State Budget. I suppose that if it works for him that the City of L.A. may follow suit. I wish you could see me laughing right now. What the hell do I have to loose. I'm taking home $22 per month after child support now is just like taking home $0 so what's the difference. I'm going down and I'm taking thousands of people with me and you're one of them. Thousands of foreclosures per quarter, we had an earthquake last week and nobody cared because there was nothing new to fall off the shelf. The unemployment lines are at it's highest calling. Banks are closing, I told my boss this was going to happen 6 months ago and he explained so enthusiastically how I was wrong. The gas companies make $15,000 per second so now is the time folks. Lets join in on the destruction. All our creditors will understand—don't worry, spend. Spend like a dog in heat; in fact I've got my wife out right now spending right now she thinks its out of love but I'm just trying to help her learn under the real system for herself. I think she's beginning to like the new me, spend it all system. By the time this book is published you will understand what I mean as some of you will no doubt be victims of these very words. So why say anymore! This book ends here!

9/07/08—Wrapped tight—that's what she did. I went to another attorney regarding getting my child support payments lowered. He said that since the court case was issued from out of state there is nothing he could do. I would have to go back to Colorado to try and get help.

9/14/08—Spoke with my daughter Simone today. Just decided to take a step and call her. She sounded happy; the recession has affected her to. She is looking for work. I could have sworn the last time I talked to her she said she had her own company. Never mind, I understand, this world is giving everybody brain failure. My only real regret is that she will never know how truly sorry I am and that I do love her.

10/03/08—So interesting to live in this time and space. The stock market is falling; unemployment is at an all time high. Watching history as a black man runs for president. Everywhere I go people need something, strange though, the recession is having an eerie effect on drivers. There is very little courtesy on

the roads today. Daily I get the finger or
am honked at. I was so curious that I asked
my wife if she was noticing the same thing.
She had just been given the finger herself. I
don't understand it but it's true. Along with
the agitation of trying to make ends meet is
the stronger will to survive, this may also
lead to a subconscious action to take control
over other human beings in preparation for the
kill and taking what they have in order to
survive.

4/11/09—I'm not writing I just wanted to look
at the pages and reminisce. Things haven't
changed much. I still work in L.A. as an Audio
Visual Technician, my wife and I are more in
love than my last entry. I flipped again, I
decided to get out of debt again and as of
this date I owe money to two of my 35 credit
cards. Cindy wants a house and word is that now
is the time because of the recession. These
are hard times. I've never seen this before,
but back to debt. I still pay the $1000 per
month child support but it doesn't hurt any
more especially since my daughter and I have
established some form of communication after
25 years. What helps is to convince my self
that I'm paying off the loan for her master's
degree.

The Video Production Business has come to
a complete halt but what is interesting
is another form of production has come to
flourishing and even overflowing to the brim.
Acting—for whatever reasons my acting skills
have blossomed and even generated funds. Last
year Cindy and I grossed $6000 with our video
production company. The prior year I think

it was something like $3000. And the year
before that it was $600. As of this date just
four months into the New Year we have grossed
nearly $6000 with $3500 of that just this
month. Churches are paying for custom skits.
Productions written in theme of the pastors'
sermon for the day enhance the atmosphere
and the audience loves it. I produced a show
last week. Long story short I was asked to
write the Easter play. When I submitted it
for approval the Minister of Music had a big
problem with it. He spent the next three weeks
using my theme and re-writing it. Instead of
complaining I went with his rendition. I had
major problems to overcome as I worked with
technical support and the actors. The only
difficulty after starting the rehearsals and
set design was to understand the script. We
got through it; last night was the last show
as it ran for three days. Let me say while it
is on my mind that, the pastor has asked that
I fill out an application for employment. I
have done so and when asked my fee for coming
on as a full time employee I indicated $75,000
per year.

This would offer me the chance to retire from
LAPD and devote my full attention to the
production needs of the church.

I was told that that would be acceptable but to
this date I have not heard from the senior pastor
regarding the job offer. He keeps requesting
stage and script and I just keep sending him
the bill. That's not so bad because on an
average they do a production once a week. It is
to my benefit that I am a private contractor.
He would be saving money if he hired me full

time. My wife is so good, she goes with me on tours as other churches have gotten wind of this phenomenon and we are now traveling by request to churches out side of the Inland Empire. Next week is in Los Angeles where I will do the one man skit 'The Bullet'. It is a rendition of the bullet that took the life of Dr. Martin Luther King Jr. You can see this performance on Youtube searching Stevensloan09 under 'THE BULLET'. God is a big part of our lives and I find myself listening to his voice as to what direction to turn on and off the set. I have been told that these performances will go nation wide. I will be performing at a Country Club requested by a church member who saw me perform a few months ago. I never set a charge just ask for an offering. I still teach an acting class at our church in Rancho Cucamonga and it seems to grow each time I do a performance. I'm tired now but I need to work on a feature film I've written so let me say fair well for now my friend.

4/30/09—Want to see something. Something you've never seen before? Let me show you what I've learned. Today I signed the papers to retire from LAPD. In complete confidence and a comfort from the voice within. The timing is perfect—that moment that I have felt on so many occasions and have been right. Or wrong never the less God tells me that I will move into a position of great authority. Have you ever felt that way? That you were so sure about something that you just moved on it. What will my wife say; my pay at this point will be cut to half of my present income from LAPD. Cindy wants a house, why didn't I buy the house and then retire? That would have been the safe thing to do. That would have been the normal thing to do. Aha! But this is not normal. Working in the spirit world is never something you would normally do. It's called faith. Lots of people talk about it but very few really know how to use it. Faith is absolute comfort when you know the odds are against you. Yes one man at the ministry says he is leaving but to retire on a single man's word is not normal. Yes the assistant pastor says it's a done deal but I've been here before and let down before. Its not that at all, it's what God says inside. He asked me if I'm ready to experience his greatest direction for me (not in those exact words). I said yes. Cindy and I have been praying for two days that the right doors be opened and the wrong doors be closed. I was talking to God today and he said move quickly. That's why I went to the retirement office and signed the papers. I get the impression that the opportunities for the man leaving the church, the one who's place I will be taking has been given a window of opportunity. This window will exist just long enough for me to step in then something will go wrong, the doors will close unless I react. He will attempt to come back but it will be to late. Have I said these words before and made a fool of myself. It seems so, yes, it was about the child support but that was not God speaking, that was me speaking. In these times only a fool would walk off a good job. Or someone who is being trained by a higher power.

5/1/09—The pastor's secretary calls our number. How did he get the number, I've only even seen him face to face one time. She says that the Pastor would like to talk to me. Cindy answered the phone so I don't know the full story but he wants to talk to me between services on Sunday. We will be there anyway; I'm supposed to be in the television production room observing the taping processing of both morning services. 28 more days to retirement, my world is about to change. We checked on the possibility of purchasing a home. We're ok with the credit but no down payment. Realtor says we need $10,000.

5/3/09—I go to the television control room to watch the process of tapping the service. 'Hello Steven' says the voice in the dark. It's the Pastor's personal secretary. She hugs me and says 'I hope he will have a chance to talk to you between services'. Hope—what do you mean hope! You called me remember, you're the one who said he wanted to talk to me. The service is over; I just know that if I go out onto the stage he will be greeting people. One hour to go before the next service starts and I wait patiently in the dark. I notice he has no time limit in talking to the people who are lined up to have a few words with him. I see his bodyguards around him trying to be discreet and the one who contacted me says what a wonderful Easter production we did.

Only 30 minutes to go, I watch patiently as he finishes up with the last person. He turns and walks away with his entourage. The officer looks back at me and kindly says maybe he forgot. At least I know I didn't miss him looking for me. I return to my seat in the television control room but someone is seating there. While relocating my things one of the assistant pastors comes in, points his finger at me and motions me to follow. Once outside he says 'Steve the pastor wants to talk to you but he doesn't want to talk about employment. He wants a skit for Mother's Day. Along the way he asks how I would feel about leaving LAPD. I explain, 'what do you mean'? Pastor I've given notice, I've signed the papers to retire'. He stops, 'WHAT', Steve you should never have done that, not until everything was confirmed. My heart stops for a moment, what have I done. Wait just a cotton picking minute buddy—You're the one who told me everything looked good (don't you just love it when people side step you like that). Once inside the building we go up the stairs. It's different here; things seem to be getting a little plusher. Approaching the huge double doors they seem to have a strong desire to gobble you up and burp. The first thing I notice is the clothing spread all over the back of the nice plushy couch, those are clothes I saw on the television monitors, they're his clothes. Then I recognize the figure sunken deep within the soft cushions. 'Hello Steven, come in, have a seat'. He knows my name. Shirttail out, shoes lying in the corner across the room, I feel as if I've invaded the privacy of his own living room. All my rehearsal about working for the ministry and God goes down the tubes. All those visions about how I was going to change the world with my dreams of music, song, drama and dance. This is a test right? A test to see if I can come up with a skit on the fly. Yes—that's it, Mother's day is next week. If I do good at coming up with something I will have passed the test. But wait a minute, it's not up to me, he is the one making the decisions as to what is to happen, it's his stage but that's okay because in my world that's called improv. Forget what you want for now Steve just make sure you get all the information from the Pastor so you can get to proving yourself then maybe in the distant future he'll hire you. 'What would you like to talk about' the pastor's question catches me off guard. I thought he was supposed to be telling me what kind of skit he wanted. I open my mouth without hesitation. How could he depend on somebody who stumbles over words? What comes out even shocks me. 'Sir I've made a mistake'. After speaking with your assistant pastor regarding employment with this ministry I gave my job at LAPD retirement notice. I've signed the papers. At first concerned then he smiles slightly 'I was aware that one day you would retire from your job but I didn't realize the time had come' he says looking at his assistant that got me into this predicament. I keep my mouth shut; this is usually the time when people talk when they shouldn't. He looks me in the eyes and spoke words that forced me to speak. 'How much'? I don't remember if I swallowed before or after but somewhere the words came out. Seventy-five thousand dollars. 'When would you want to start'? Tuesday May 12ᵗʰ I say with spit still lingering behind my tongue. He looks at his assistant pastor sitting next to me. 'Make it happen'. Then I swallow.

5/29/09—At midnight tonight it's all over. No turning back, the retirement will be final. Will not get my monthly $1900 check for life until 30 days after that. It's actually $2900 per month but $1000 goes to child support.

That's a good thing. I will be 70 years old when it is paid off but I'm on God's time so what's right is going to happen.

6/1/09—Two weeks on the new job. The small retirement party last week still lingers in my head but I just couldn't find the erg to cry. I ate and said good-bye. It feels good. There's a strange piece of paper in my box at the church. I open it up! It's a check for $3100. I will get this every two weeks. God is real.

6/5/09—They called me in from the retirement office. My retirement is on HOLD! What! That's right—you heard me. Lost at sea without an ore. Not really, I'm well taken care of, in fact; the retirement check has become chump change. What's the hold up?

My divorce, I mean divorces. Okay so I've married numerous times. In the bible men had wives and concubines so what's the deal? Alright; alright, the deal is that in this country you are looked upon as a strange animal if you have been married more than twice. Preachers talk about it all the time in congregations across the land; 'Ya sinner! Look at cha. Can't get your life right. Sitting around waiting for a hand out. You're smoking, drinkin, ya been married numerous times. Look at yourself, what's wrong with you that you can't keep a wife. I'll tell you what you need. You need Jesus'. Let me tell you something Mr. preacher. I had Jesus all those times that I was married and even on one occasion I prayed to Jesus to get me out of the marriage so there. I got an appointment to see the Retirement people on Monday we'll find out what this is all about.

6/8/09—So I walk in with a stack of files under my arm and the lady I had an appointment with was not working on today. This guy walks in and introduces himself as the legal analyst. He explains 'I'm the guy who determines whether or not your retirement check should be sent to your ex-wife or not'! Noooooooooooo! Not a gain! I can't stand this. That guy who wrote that song should be put in the Hall of Fame. What was it again—oh yeah! 'It's Cheaper to Keep her'. What do you mean give, give, give. By the way, speaking of giving I was so excited last Saturday when I went to work the Saturday Night service to write that check for $300 and place it in the offering tray for tithes, had not been able to do that in a long time. It really feels good to serve such an awesome God. Now back to my complaining. What do you mean give to my ex-wife. He shuffles through all the files and determines that only one wife could possibly apply to qualifying to share my retirement funds. The file will be sent to the City Attorney who will make the determination as to what percentage she should receive. If anywhere on the divorce decree it states that my ex-wife should get a cretin percentage of the retirement dispersement it will be included as a deduction. I clearly remember what those papers said and there was no such language to my knowledge. But wait a minute Steve—remember the last time you got jacked. Remember the $1000 child support deduction? God gave you more money than you were making prior to the judgment. So come on with it. Come on wives lets get it on. All of you get together and have an ex-husband alimony party. In fact, I'll get you one attorney to handle me. I'm getting this; I'm starting to understand something. No matter what your situation, as long as your heart is right, as long as you maintain a relationship with Jesus in prayer and commitment to at least try to live your life helping people come to the understanding of his word. As long as you look to him in faith, each and every day to supply your needs, wham bam—nothing that happens to you is going to destroy you. People look for ways to take from you. And unfortunately sometimes even your own family. Looking, seeking opportunity to pull you back down into the crab barrel and onto the ground, even under the ground to your grave. It's true you guys, it works, God works. It's not just words or something on T.V. you have to master it but it's worth so much more than school or a degree. It means much more to work for God's purpose. I'm just going to kick it, let God deal with this retirement stuff. I'm tired of complaining. Besides, I was just commissioned to write and produce five commercials for the BET Awards coming up in two weeks. How is God going to pull this one off?

6/26/09—Odd, each week it's something new. A new skit, a different script yet they want more. I ask Cindy 'What am I, is this what all writers are doing'? She asks me what I mean and I tell her I didn't know. Now every other week I perform before the Wednesday night pastor speaks. One week prior to his sermon I get the title of his message. One week after that, I'm displaying to the audience what the pastor is about to talk about as a theatrical performance.

Haven't started writing the Christmas play and the script and budget is due on the 1st of July. I was able to film three commercials in the past two weeks. They are all on television including 5 produced especially for BET to be aired on the 28th during the BET Awards. The New Year's Eve script is due but not as important as Christmas. Got to get to work on it. I have an Idea for a showcase, yeah, that might be fun. Today is the appointment to see the realtor. Should be interesting, American Express Card came two weeks ago, in the wife's name but it's ours, this is what I've been waiting for all my life. Got the first bill already. $800, I paid $1000. Should be interesting. I put last weeks Wednesday Night performance on You Tube. It's called 'When Evil Prevails'. Favor with God is a good thing. (Search Youtube for Stevensloan09)

7/9/09—I don't understand. They come at me from all directions. The ministry without a conscience. Requesting scripts, mini films, music song and dance. The Christmas script was due last week and I just proofread the first six pages. That was the sum total of the entire work. I asked around if anyone knew of a time management course I could get involved with. They laugh. Why can't I at least catch up? I have to stay sane. Look around you Steve, focus. I can't do this, I can't continue like this. Is this what they call overwhelmed. What do you do when people depend on you so overwhelmingly? The Pastor will be back from vacation next week. I thought I could catch up on editing while he was gone but no! The staff gang jumped me and requested more shows and lights; camera; action. I need to write the music for the play, I work better when I can hear the atmosphere, see my characters then write them in. I need to write the script for next Wednesday. The Pastor is back; the scene is for his sermon. It's about healing, what about healing? I messed up; I was told by the bookstore that they needed a commercial. I made it five minutes instead of thirty seconds. We shot all day Saturday and now what? I messed up. My wife is having a fit, I forgot what she looks like. I have to cut it down to thirty seconds. I'm gonna put it on You Tube. Went through all that for nothing. I'll call it 'The Book Signing'. Relax Steve, at least you made another film.

8/4/09—Applied for a Home loan. We've had American Express for about a month now. Wait till they get a load of me. I had been trying to get a card for 30 years. They seem to think that we may qualify for something, the house loan that is. I went online and filled out the application. We want to move closer to the Church. Rancho Cucamonga is the game plan. I wanted to document this occasion, God's timing. The Loan people are confused about our 2007 taxes and quite frankly—so are we. We tried to use TurboTax. We made like, one million dollars on paper and tried to get three million back, this of course due to the software learning curve. Nevertheless we just jacked it up. IRS had to finish the documents for us. We ended up getting three thousand back from State and Federal. I think I talked about this previously for the actual figures. Anyway, since Cindy and I have been married God's timing in every situation has prevailed. Because this is such an important step for us,

I figures that we are really going to see the results of His timing. Testimonials verifying God's timing. What would it have been like if Moses would have been able to show a video to his people weeks or months prior to them leaving the land as to how the waters would part to let them by. Watch these waters part.

It will take us at least two months to get copies from IRS. We never saw the forms they had to complete for us. Loan company says get the W2s from our employers but, wouldn't we still have to pay someone to do our taxes?

By the way we are expert TurboTax users now. What a pain to go around collecting all those documents. We can get it from IRS in one clean shot.

Check this out, remember I talked about the guy whose place I took—you know the media ministry. I just found out that he was making eighty-five thousand, I got ripped. I went in at seventy-five and I'm working not one ministry like he was but three. What was I thinking? Sorry God—I don't know why I said that forgive me.

Our apartment lease is up in December. There is a penalty for checking out early. Is anybody getting this? Why should we be anxious for anything? We have four months before our house will be built or before the people in our house will be notified that they have to move. It would be easy to get so excited about your first house, car, boat, plane but the experience we have gained so far is such that we know how the water will part. This timing thing—now that's what is exciting. What a life, to know that you will never miss you calling, your destiny is preprogrammed. You're a video game already to be played out in everyday situations. You're a slot machine with people pouring wealth into you and every now and then you reward someone else.

With that my friend I must thank you for your time is reading his book. It's quite obvious that with the house we will not be getting out of debt. That is unless God wants to make another timing move. After we sign the papers I will conclude this journey. So for those of you who are still in your cars and no desire to purchase a home. You can get little fly screen at the auto parts store; they will keep the fly's out during the summer time. Despite my success, I have greatly failed you. There you are waiting till dark to use the restroom and I have enough room to put you and your car in mine. No need to read any further my friend. If you read this book within 30 days of purchase you should have no problem returning it for a refund. I'm sorry I let you down, I'll be praying for you. Bye!

8/27/09—After several contacts from the mortgage company regarding things we needed yet to submit for the house loan, a final message saying that all necessary paperwork was in and has been submitted to final preparation of loan approval. We never got upset at all the inconveniences. Most people would have gotten upset or even given up by now but when you know that every delay is being orchestrated by God and his will and timing, we laughed at all the details that told us that the loan would not go through. A new guy has been hired to take my place in the Media Ministry at church, which takes a load off me. There is still talk of me working in the Drama Ministry and now the Television Ministry keeping the churches commercials up to date. As for now, I am still over Media, Drama, and Television Production. I did some research regarding the pay scale for these positions and the combined—excuse me but I was just interrupted by a pastor who needs me to film a commercial about a kid in a bathtub be right back . . . Believe it or not in about three weeks this commercial will have something to do with ministering to people. Is this great or what? This is everyday and sometimes twice that people need excuse me again—I hope your sitting down because what I'm about to tell you is incredible. As I was writing you these words about the house loan, the mortgage company called. Mind you, I am on my lunch break. I never write during lunch only at night at my leisure.

The mortgage company called to tell me that we had been approved to $400,000. I instantly called my wife to let her the exciting news. God and his timing. What a privilege to be able to hear the voice of God say 'sit down and write in your journal'. Can you comprehend what just happened? I'm sitting here writing about God's time when God proves his timing while I'm writing about his timing. Is that God or what? I gotta get back to work before I start crying. I'm going to be late—please, grab hold of the life with Jesus Christ. I've never lied to you intentionally or intended to deceive you. I joke around a lot but you must realize. What just happened is a miracle.

Not the house, I knew that was going to happen through faith. But you holding this book in your hand right have just witnessed a modern day miracle. God is trying to tell you something with these simple words. With this simple experience. If he can make you have an experience—excuse me—The pastor of the church that time. He called to tell me about a film he wants shot for this weekend. I really got to go I'm late for a shoot. Please consider what I just said my friend. If I get a chance tonight when I get off I will write talk to you. Good by!

9/5/09—Yesterday! Our three-year anniversary. Want to guess what I bought Cindy? I'll give you a hint. It's bigger than a shoebox and you can live in it. About three weeks ago Cindy and I went to visit a realtor. She was very nice and a member of our church. I was unable to make the appointment to visit a few houses to establish our possibilities. Cindy was so excited that night to tell me about the model homes she had visited. One particular house was everything she had wanted. She left that day telling the realtor that she didn't think that I would like it because it had practically no room to build in the back yard for our prop house. I agreed with her when she expressed her findings at our apartment that night. I told her that I would take a chance and look around on my own for a better selection. I started looking on the Internet and I became frustrated at the findings.

I drove to the mortgage company and explained my frustration and that I was unable to find a listing under their name.

The rep said that there was only one house left
and that they would start land development on
new phases in January. He told me I could visit
the builder. I drove around for two days on my
lunch breaks and was never able to find the
builder. Finally I just refused to stop looking
for it. I found it and walked through the model
homes. I only found one that I liked. I went
back and told my wife that I, the great one
had found our new home. When I described it to
her she began to laugh. She asked if we could
go by and see it. The next day we were at the
front door. Several people had wanted to buy
the house but they had not been pre-approved.
To my amazement—it was the exact same house
she had visited almost a month ago. We wrote
the check and on Tuesday I'm to replace the
check with a cashier's check. Need I try to
explain once again the aspect of God's timing?
When I went to the builder I had no idea that
Cindy had been there previously nor the house
she liked. Several empty boxes await us in the
garage of our current apartment because when
I started praying for the house we started
collected empty boxes to move. I don't know if
you get it or not. Do you understand what has
happened? I think I may have mentioned to you
about God's Timing. Patience—we had patience
with God and were available to listen. You
have to prepare yourself to hear God's voice.
It's about your life style that gets you over.
There is still a long ways to go and we aren't
perfect but you have to see what is happening.
This thing is too big not to say something
about it. God and His awesome timing.

9/14/09—A word from God. 'I want you to know
how much I appreciate everything you are doing

for me and I'm going to show my appreciation through Faith and a financial blessing'. Despite my telling God that after all he's done for the human race and me that he didn't have to do anything else. He insisted that this blessing occur. I used my sick leave for the down payment on the house. The mortgage company says they have FedExed the final papers and we are to sign them and send them back. The current rate is 5.1. excuse me a moment—I'm going to call the mortgage contact and ask her what is the website that I can monitor the current interest rate, I didn't know there was such a thing. She told me that once the papers are complete that I can determine when the rate should be locked. Here we go, are you seeing any timing issues here? My guess is that at the very time that we tell her to lock the interest rate, it will be the lowest ever in history and only for a very short time. I'll be right back . . . She says the rate as of Friday was 5.125. The paperwork will be here on Wednesday. My wife and I have to work on Wednesday so we will not be here to receive the package that is so important. You want to know what's exciting about working with God. You never know how He plans to succeed in achieving your goal. There should be a commercial like the ones we have heard so many times regarding joining the military. You know—'be all that you can be' and stuff like that. By the way, you should see the beautiful keyboard God allowed me to have to produce the music for the play. Hand Of A Friend will be performed at the church on Dec 16th through the 18th. I'm sure I will be talking about that later. Where was I? Oh yeah! The commercial. This guy is lying on a white sandy beach. We

HEAR the cool winds blowing and the rhythm of the ocean waves. He looks to the skies and smiles saying, 'It probably looks like I'm on vacation. But in reality I'm hard at work. With everyday challenges, family affairs, economical problems, dreams and desires, but if it doesn't look like I'm worried about it. I'm not, you see, I've learned to relax in Jesus and let him do all the work. Now that was off the head my friend, I think I'll go get my camera.

I just wanted to talk to you and let you see the effects of God in my life. Talk to you soon.

CHAPTER 24

THE EVIDENCE OF PRAYER

9/28/09—I want you to see something. Quickly—here my voice on this date it is 1:50pm. I just received a call from the builders of our home. Sure we went through some challenges and I do apologize that I did not get back to tell you what God was doing. I just wanted you to experience a miracle in real time. The builder just called—wait let me back up. On Thursday of last week as I was on my way to the DV Expo in Pasadena I pulled over to accept a call. It was a representative from the builders. He said that he had made an appointment for us to do a walk through at the house on Friday October 2nd at 9am. I was so excited to call Cindy and tell her. By the time she got home she had told everyone at work. Hold on now let me catch my breath. So you got that information right? Well on this date I just received not 10 minutes ago a call from that very person whom by the way is named JESUS. I told my wife the other night how it was that God would lead us individually to the same house and now we were being given a tour by Jesus himself. Any way—that phone call I just received from Jesus sounded confused. The builder asked if I was the one who changed the appointment to the weekend. I said no. The sales guy handed the phone to Jesus. He said when was our appointment. I said 'stop right there' you are not going to hurt my wife by trying to change the situation. He said that there may have been a mistake about the property. I told him not in so many words that I'm not saying anything to my wife and he better be right.

He said he would call the builders and call me back. Well that's not the issue. I don't care about the house or the words spoken or the immature phone call. By the way I did ask Jesus what went wrong. How could he get peoples hopes up like this and then say it was a mistake. Excuse me a moment. I just went into the kitchen of our apartment to turn the meat and I asked God If I should call the loan people and say that I just received a call from the builders and they say there is a problem and how do we get our money back. God said just leave it alone 'I'm working on your prayer'. You see as soon as I hung up with Jesus I went into heavy prayer. I'm talking tongues binding the devil, confessing favor with the builders and that the situation will change to our favor and that is our house and the Devil is defeated. I get this feeling of comfort inside and that is what God said. Please understand that rarely will you have an opportunity to experience how God works in this way to understand how to grasp you life to the fullest extent. To make a long story short and let my fingers rest, my story stops there. I want you to see God work. I want you to see that God answers the prayers of the righteous. You have got to get this. It's not a game, as these words are written the future is only known by God. Let me tell you what is about to happen. This guy Jesus is going to call me ant tell me that the appointment is still on, not to tell my wife anything. In reality can you see? Knowing the voice of God is in your favor. What do you need to prove it except manifestation. Who else do you need to say it to you? God wants to do things in your life. He wants you to see miracles. Don't try to tell me different now that I'm a man sitting here writing words that have not come to pass yet. How many books have you read where the outcome is prophesized and in progress? My friends excuse me while I catch my breath. The man has not called me back yet and I telling you what he is going to say. Oh you say, anybody can do that. Anyone can say what they want to here, but there is only one problem with that. You-know-me! I would never deceive you. I'm waiting for the call, if it comes today or tomorrow this comfort in my spirit over rides any information that the world can produce. May I take a moment to tell you why the opposition would not like it if we purchased the house? It's my entire fault. As I watched the videotape I took of the house as I visited a few weeks ago, I noticed one small bedroom. It's only about 12' X 12' and a little closet. I'm sure it was meant to be a guest room. Anyway I said to myself—self, that is going to be the Altar Room. The place where my wife and me go to visit God. The replacement of the rocks stacked in the biblical days to represent the faithfulness of God. The place where we will spend every morning praying to the God who gave us such a blessing and strength, life, love, happiness. That is going to be the hub of the neighborhood and I will constantly look for ways to make it beautiful to God. If I would never had spoken those words out loud to my wife maybe Satan would not have eased dropped, then we would not be having this opposition. But remembering the words of the scriptures that say that nothing will be experienced that you cannot handle. When things get tough it's because you have graduated. I await the call to give you the good news. My spirit senses some minor discomfort. That means that things will work out but there is some technical issue.

3:20pm just received a call from Jesus. The meeting to do our walk through is on for Friday at 9am. What further evidence do you need?

10/02/09—The enemy strikes subtly. We have a walk through this morning at 9am. It was canceled a couple of times but not by us. The Builder made a mistake and got us confused with someone else. Constant prayer that the original appointment would be kept has been the only reason we go this morning. We still don't know the out come of the leaking brick wall. Our research shows that it's something called infiltration or something like that. It's where the concrete looses some of its strength due to water seeping through the pores. That wall doesn't look as nice. The builder says they will talk to the lady who owns the property next door to us. We're starting off good in the neighborhood—complaining.

There's something else. I was called to the office two days ago. My supervisor at the church says he will be discussing hiring someone to head the Media Department. This would allow me to go back to working the required 47 hours a week instead of 50-60. The bad news is that he would cut my pay from $75,000 down to $65,000 and would that be acceptable. I expressed my sincere appreciation for the opportunity to serve God and to use my creative skills for the ministry and accepted. Mind you—there was a verbal agreement that came with the original offer. 'A two year commitment, two feature play productions, head the Media and Drama departments'. Since that agreement an additional ministry was added, Television Production of the church commercials. Those extra duties were not considered for an increase. As of right now I average 55 hours a week with 77 hours of compensation time on the books. I mentioned earlier that the enemy attacks subtly; yesterday I was called into the office again. My supervisor said that the pastor made a mistake. My pay cut is now down to $60,000. Until then or at least until the new guy is hired I remain at $75,000. Am I complaining? Yes—not about the reduction in pay. People tell you anything when they are in trouble. I was hired because there was no one else who could do the job. Now that there are going to be two people under me one of them will take my place. There was never a contract but I can't remember ever signing a contract to be hired for a job. I just trusted the employer. Still—these are heard times and $60,000 a year is very suitable for an actor and keys to a 4000 seat auditorium.

Though there is some embarrassment. I use to be an excellent witness at the police station. Everyone knew that if you serve God and try to live your life the right way he will reward you with more money than the Police Department would be able to pay. Any lower than $60,000 and I would attempt to avoid any conversation with my old friends so not to have to expose the fact that things aren't as stable working for a church as I boosted.

In order to complete our closing papers the loan officer requires proof of homeowners insurance. The insurance company called a couple of days ago and said they could not give us insurance for the house because of our video business. Somehow they got the impression that we were opening up a theater in our home. A few hours of prayer was my lunch that day. When the loan office gets wind that we cannot get insurance they say for me to try to find insurance and to be discreet as to our business. I had inquired before as to why I couldn't use AAA as my insurer but I was told that 'unless you use the loan office insurance that all special deals were off and we would have to come up with an additional $20,000 for closing. Some how their heart was softened and they found a way to accept my suggestion to go with homeowners insurance at AAA. Cindy and I eat prayer for lunch quite often these days. You don't suppose that the Pastor cut my pay because the loan office had to verify my pay do you? My word from God, is to move quickly, that this season will not last much longer.

The idea of the eagle's nest seems to be very apparent to me right now. With each pay cut it represents feathers being extracted from my nest. At the thought of making $65,000 I began to feel the discomfort of being vulnerable to the system. Held victim to a single human being taking from me security for my family and me. Then at $60,000 a little more pain that whispers in my ear to not be slave to man. God says now is the time to build your empire. Unless you are in charge of your destiny someone else may wipe away your dreams. Cindy is through with the pastor. Ever since she became aware that the life style of the podium is different than the staff meetings than the reality of the life lived by the man behind it. Warfare exists. Strategically plan my attack. Accept the fire darts and extinguish them secretly so no one knows you are injured. Meanwhile build your own fort, train your own warriors behind the walls. Be careful of spies because if you are found out, what little fortitude you have will be taken away completely and you will be destroyed being found unprepared. The enemy will look for weaknesses in your financial situation. When you over come one thing the pressure will increase. Remember that nothing is new. These problems have happened to you before only under different circumstances. The only true victory comes through prayer. The advantage the enemy has is that he has been fighting for thousands of years and you, well, just know that you have more power that you think, you just have to know how to use it. Your weapon is prayer—giving the situation to God. Praying to Him about how you would like for things to turn out and ask Him to take the helm, because you can't do it without Him. Faith is your bullets. The stronger your faith that everything will be handled and work out, the more powerful the effects of your ammunition. Life is never easy but if you have to deal with deceitful people, unsure circumstances, situations in which you have no or very little control. You need a friend like God.

10/08/09—I couldn't sleep. Having faith doesn't mean that you don't experience the worry of life's issues. The pastor has a problem with the script I submitted yesterday. October 16th is the dead line to have the paper work in or the show does not go on. The budget must be signed before the paper work can be submitted. There lye the problems. The Pastor will not sign the budget until at least four other people have read the script. He didn't understand the pitch I gave. I admit, I am hard to under-stand; it's just this darn imagination of mine. I don't always understand what I'm doing until all is said and done. Then people say 'Wow you're a genius'. I have given the script 'Hand of A Friend' to the four perspective judges and will meet with the pastor next week. He held the 115-page document in his hand. He felt the weight of months of working on my days off. In my mind I thought how can a person wave such a document around and not be aware of all the hard work that was put into writing it? Did the words from this script just appear? I think not—nevertheless, his interpretation of how I described the play took on a whole new meaning. As a writer I'm well aware that once submitted to different parents your baby is birthed and comes out looking different than when first conceived but where was your interpretation during conception. There are people who simply must put in there two cents in every good idea. To be involved in the pat on the back but never gets the brainstorm until someone else builds the foundation first. But who's complaining, I kept track of every hour spent writing the script. Though it seems to be a donation to the church simply because in most cases I was off duty, the comp time lays Dorset on my log. The pastor told me yesterday that he has no intentions of hiring me to do the television production once they replace me in Media. He is going to out source the job. Hire someone to produce the commercials

for television. In his words let the media
department handle the commercials. Can you say
Green Screen? That is not television and that
is all the ministry has to offer. You need a
filmmaker to make commercials for television.
Those few words are what sat me in front of
this screen. I am in the media department; I
am a filmmaker yet 'I' was excluded from the
process. Are you getting something here? I'm
about to be terminated.

You have to look at the big picture, listen to
words and trust your intuition. Let me tell
you a story. Back in 1985 I was an announcer
for a gospel radio station with its remote
transmitter located on Colorado Boulevard in
the city of Pasadena California. The drive on
the freeway gave me opportunity to pray. To
spend time thanking God for the day and most of
all my radio show. On this particular morning
at about 4:00am I was going through my ritual
when God told me 'I'm going to do something
I've never done with you before' maybe not
in those exact words but I got the message.
Jokingly I replied 'So what are you going to
do Lord, make me float around the studio'?
There was no reply and that bothered me. We
have always had open communication before.

Long story short, the answer came about an
hour later as I was on the air. God said
'I want you to tell the people that if they
lay their hands on their radio they will be
healed'. That was cool; I could follow that
command with ease only one problem. On the
day I was hired the general manager told me
that under no condition was I to pray on the
air. He made it clear that I am not paid to

pray and the only people who could pray were
the pastors that pay for airtime. I had to
remind God about those conditions. God's a
very busy man and probably just forgot. I can
disregard God's instructions but I can't fight
the spiritual fireworks that occur inside my
spirit. Tears and snot, that's what I remember
most about that morning. Bouncing off the
hallway walls praying in tongues a hard labor
yet willingness to give birth to this child of
inspiration of my orders from God. Why does
God put us though those challenges? Maybe love
is more genuine when you sacrifice for it. I
would hate to be the one to use that microphone
after me that morning. One simple click to the
transmit button and my tears were heard to a
half million people getting ready for work.

Did I say long story short? Lots of people
were healed that day. Rightfully so—I was
terminated. Oh, I almost forgot why I brought
that story up in the first place. Prior to my
labor pains God told me to remove all my personal
possessions from my radio station office. Man
you should have seen the look on the general
managers face when he had me escorted out of
the building and when we passed my office he
said don't bother to get your things we will
have them sent to you. What gratitude to see
his face when he looked in side my office to
hear his last few words echo and bounce off
the empty walls and smack him in the face.

Anyway, I'm getting the same unction. I have
a few things tucked away at the church I will
collect by the end of the week. You know what!
If I have any regret at all, it's that I involved
a very precious woman to become victim in all

of this. She does not deserve the uncertainty of not knowing if she will be able to keep her dream house. She did nothing wrong except choose me as her husband. I have done this to her and for that I ask for forgiveness from the God who gives me the unction. Yeap! Just like the tears and snot that flow right now. That's how it was that day. It's a slow kill, I'm bleeding and the hunter get his jollies from watching me die. As my tissues pile up before me, I say to myself. 'Do you have any idea how easy it is to just consider'? Consider if how you are living out your life is what you agreed to in the beginning. If your actions represent what you say. If someone else may experience pain or loose respect because of a conflict in your decisions? Life seems easier than this. Keep your word, especially you pastors out there. At least do what you say from the pulpit. Is it that hard to just do right? When the church fails us, where is there to go? When our pastors fail us, who is there to listen to? The answer is simple. Never trust in man. The only hope you have is found within yourself, lead by giving birth to the child the God had placed within you. I'm gonna blow my nose and go lay down with my wife. Thanks for helping to make me sleepy.

10/13/09—A few days ago around the ninth, my supervisor at the church called me into a private meeting. 'How much did the pastor forget to cut my pay now' I replied. He wanted to know if the Pastor had mentioned to me (after rejecting my Christmas script) that he was planning on shifting my position from being under him (my supervisor) to directly under himself (the Pastor). I said no he had

not and could he expound. He said evidently
the pastor feels that I could be of greater
benefit if I am over the Fine Arts Ministry
without being under my current supervisor.
That would place me as a director, the same as
my current supervisor. The trickery persists,
did my supervisor go to the Pastor and explain
to him how hurt I was over my pay being cut.

Let me mention something. Every Thursday
morning about thirty minutes prior to the
weekly staff meeting, myself, my supervisor
and his assistant have the most wonderful
fellowship time I have ever experienced. We
all agree that nowhere on the church campus is
the anointing so strong than when we pray to
God and ask for the manifestation of change
in the church staff for the better. On last
Thursday it was a little different for me. As
it was my turn to pray, the tears and snot just
would not stop flowing. All my inner pain and
confusion just came out in a plea for God to
help the Pastor see what he is doing to people.
That he himself is cause of any down falls and
is blind to see that some of the very things
he preaches that we (the congregation) should
not do, he himself is guilty of. And in case
that Pastor is reading this book—this is a
contradiction of your word. Telling people you
will do one thing then doing another. To be
precise, do everything to keep from breaking
your word to an employee saying that you want
a two-year contract of service.

That includes your side of the bargain. Those
two years would include keep your words as to
the amount of pay you promised also. Especially
after a person comes off of their job and into

retirement because of an offer you made to match their pay plus five thousand per year. The prayer included a change in his lack of planning, weekly administration direction and contradictions that cause the staff to bow their heads and pretend that he is making the right decision. Do you remember the story of the naked king? All the royal subjects told the king he was wearing beautiful clothing because they were afraid of loosing their head if they told him that in reality he was really butt naked. With so many compliments he began to believe it him self. It takes a very different human being to be able to look at himself in the mirror and not only ask the question as to what problems did I initiate today, who did I hurt, and admit that it was all their fault then say how can I prevent from doing that again. What could I have done to turn the outcome to a positive experience for everyone? Where do I need help? What are my weaknesses? The opposite of these are easily admitted and accepted as the prominent life style for the observer. If the person mentioned above were to hear another person openly admit these faults, they would still not conclude that maybe they have some of the same issues. Like I said, it takes very disciplined and mature people to analyze themselves and diagnose that they need help or even be willing to do something to change. By the way, I did hear that a new guy was hired to take over the Media Department so I should be expecting my pay cut but at the time of this writing, I still make the same amount that I was originally hired for.

Let's see now, where was I before I went off on a tangent and made a completed fool of myself a moment ago. Oh yes the reason I started this entry was because my wife called me sounding very excited. She said that a lady had just contacted her from some title company. She ran from her desk to call me as her phone might drop the call inside the building. I contacted the lady and as it was we were to be in her office to sign loan papers in two hours. I contacted my wife back with the information and off she went headed home. My inquiry as to who the lady was verified to me that we needed to sign loan papers pronto. During the fifty-mile journey we concluded that the people loaning us the money for the house needed to finalize our loan papers in fact, one hour worth of loan papers. I felt it odd that a loan company would have us sign so many papers that had to do with information not containing figures and payment plans but legal stuff about ownership and property and taxes and on and on. After signing all but a few pages I couldn't resist asking. 'If all this signing is for the loan I can just imagine what the closing ceremony must be like. The nice lady looked me in the eyes and smiled saying, "Congratulations Mr. and Mrs. Sloan. You have just closed on your house and you should be receiving a call from the property managers regarding picking up your keys in about two days."

Yesterday on the way to the prop house I decided to stop by the security training facility. This is where you obtain credentials to be security guard and the likes. I inquired as to how to further my education in the security field. Twenty-six hundred dollars would be a wise investment in myself. A three week course to upgrade my security skills and add value to my application should I need to look for work would be a wise investment. I'll start class after my last class of the school of ministry, in about two weeks. P.S. regarding getting the house. Everyone knows that they only approve houses for the white . . . 🔨

11/02/09—We've been in the new house now for two weeks. It's beautiful. Incredibly easy to do! We have friends who just got into a house and have been looking for two or three months before we started. They went through bidding, looking, earnest money, looking, missed appointments and late night worries. I went to look at a house, liked it, three weeks later we were at closing. Weird thing, buying a house, there are different sharks to attack you. We get strange letters now—by the way I forgot to tell you, we were able to move in to the house so fast that our first payment isn't due for six weeks. But here's the clincher. We couldn't get out of our lease at the apartment. Our lease isn't up until December 31st, which means not only that we will be paying on an apartment that we are not using but also come December 1st; we will be paying on two residences. The bible says that God will bless you with houses and cattle but I think right now I'd rather have the cows. Actually, our prayers are so thankful to God and we have faith that since he has allowed this to happen like this that he will provide.

The church did say that my pay will be cut down to $60,000 but man oh man, how many actors in Hollywood would love to make that. I'm now working on writing scene two of the Easter

Play to be performed December 16th-18th. This is a re-write, the first one was rejected. I think I have a better handle of what the pastor wants. Quite frankly he wants souls to be saved. He wants me to scare the hell out of the people who come via tears and slinging snot. He wants a Christmas story about Jesus that pulls the people down to the front stage and onto their knees. He wants a theatrical Billy Graham. I could never do this so I won't even try. I'm real excited to see how God pulls this one off. Oh yeah, about those letters you get from different sharks in the realty sea. Evidently when you purchase a house, what you paid and anything else about you becomes public information. People who were not mentioned at closing are asking for money to guarantee this; fix something, build something for you and insure that manufactures of curtains and blinds stop by to tell you of the new law that you have to have your windows covered or you will go to jail necked. I even had a guy driving around asking me if he could remove the dents from my car to make the neighborhood look more decent. I'm spending a lot of money on insurance. I know I'll be doing filming here and heaven forbid that anything happen to an actor or crew. When my wife and I talk our voices echo but in time we will have the furniture we need. To save a little money the plan is to move everything out of the prop house and bring it here. That will be a savings of just under $300 per month. But do we have room you ask. 3 floors, 5 bed rooms (one we turned into an office) 1 master bath with separate shower and Jacuzzi, Kitchen/Family room, Living room, Dining room, three car garage, oh and get this film students—the third floor has only one room—a theater. One of the bedrooms is being made into an altar room. Can you get to that, the smallest bedroom is going to be a place to study about God. Who do I think I am some kind of priest or something? If the pastors at church heard about this they would laugh me out of the city. 'The nobody—want to be actor thinking he could be in touch with the same God we preach about'. Now that takes guts for me to pull this one off. You know me by now. You know my heart. I've poured my soul out to you in the last few years. Then you know that for me to get from where I was to where I am now, it happened supernaturally. There was a plan for my life that was not totally clear to me. Still I hear further promotion down the line like recognition like I've never known. That's what God is saying; 'I'm going to set you in a higher place'.

How to handle fame and keep your head by remembering where you came from. Hey that's not a bad title for a book. Speaking of books, how can words express how much I appreciate you taking time to read these thoughts of mine. I started this book off by trying to be some kind of know it all about sleeping in your car and getting out of debt. I proved myself a liar by never having achieved the goal. Now with the house and my pay cut I should be able to keep it together but with a $3000 per month mortgage I just don't see any reason for continuing this book unless I change the name to something like 'Your roof—Your debt'. I'm ending my story a failure in my eyes. If you're smart enough to recognize that there are several more pages to this book don't worry about turning this last page. The rest of them are blank. It just goes to show that just because you start a race doesn't mean that you will finish, but at least you got in the race. So farewell my friend, get your money back from buying this book and go see a movie.

Sincerely: Steve Sloan

1/20/10—I missed you! At times there was no one to talk to. Though I tried to end this conversation, on this date the thought of you over powered me. Hi, just wanted to tell you how much I love you. Today pain exists inside me. The church isn't happy with my work. It's so weird, I'm doing the very best I can and now the question is asked 'what are we paying this guy for'. You know what that means. The pastor asked me to produce a commercial on Friday morning. After writing the script, casting, arranging a location, gathering equipment, filming then editing all night, the commercial was not ready for Saturday Night's service. When people look for excuses that you failed that's when you know your assignment is over and it's time to move on. I started writing another book about the people I work with at the church. Want to read it? I only wrote a few pages. Let me copy and paste, I feel comfortable sharing it with you, you're my only friend. It's kind of strange but you know me by now. Here it is.

CHAPTER 25

THE SHADED LIGHT

IN THE MISTS OF A SHADED LIGHT
By Steve Sloan

Within the organization of any ministry there are people who are called by God. They are the light that stands before the congregation. They contain the light that shines outward and is collected by the spirits of those who come to attend. This light is projected by music & song, dance, drama even preaching itself, yet unbeknown to the proprietor; the light is shaded by mental deception generated by a self-centered current meant for illumination.

How is it that we don't see who we really are? In most cases we only recognize the limited image reflected in the mirrors of our own minds, heaven forbid the ones on our bathroom walls. Yet to walk in self-deception is a zombie state of mind somehow accepted by the ignorance of others and recognized occasionally by a few.

Those few who dare to acknowledge the shaded light have little options. To exist within the light or expel themselves only to find the light shines in all parts of other ministries as well. These few, if not devoured by the shaded light, become victims with only one option to survive. To pretend to be shaded them selves. Despite the association of the shaded light there is an advantage of knowing the zombie exists but is not seeking to destroy you because of your awareness. One question holds true. This calling by God to those who illuminate the congregation; knowing the shade exists; but God still chooses to allow their light to shine, for the shade is only recognized by a few and people do get saved despite man's personal definition of deception.

What is it to recognize the shade, what would then be projected if the zombie suddenly saw his own reflection? The opportunity to see ones self occurs when other lights describe the existence of the down falls of the zombie walk. Yet somehow the exposure of the shaded light is dismissed as someone else's dilemma not their own. The mirror is fogged by the hot waters of self-esteem. It covers the body like a cocoon and is only washed away when one searches within ones self in an attempt to expose the zombie within.

If the zombie is found it is for the better. He will never be removed only changed at heart. He becomes aware that there may be other zombies living within the organization. The search continues the hunter for his pray. To hack ones self-seeking spiritual weakness is the endeavor of the few. It's an observation that does not come without the penalty of backbiters or laughter on the other side of an attentive face. The zombie will not recognize himself, only those who refuse to participate, thus, the option of pretending to be one.

Beyond the ignorance of the light, blessings unfold despite the shade. God uses the light for His will and removes the shade with His anointing. Yet when the cloud moves and the smoke and flame dissipates, the zombie re-appears as his old reflection regurgitates behind the shadow of the shaded light.

In most cases a zombie can only be identified as you have access to the territory of which he breeds. You must at least spend time with the zombie to observe his communication of ideas, mannerism and speech. You must be in a position to observe the zombie carry out his intentions verses in order to prepare yourself to survive the end result. His intentions will soon transform into a shade of contradiction and the end result, a search for an escape to get himself out of trouble should his identity be compromised. The time it takes for you to identify the zombie depends on your experience in having a watchful eye, and good memory or journal and be constantly on the lookout for opportunity to observe and identify the true intention. It is not necessary to physically live with a zombie to study their shading in fact, those who do live with the zombie are deeply shaded due to several obstructions which prevent them from seeing the light. For instance: <u>Love</u> for the zombie will shade the light of reality and will rarely transform into a means of helping the zombie shed the shade. <u>Fear</u> of the zombie will keep the mouths of other observant zombies from acknowledging the zombie's shade he needs to shed. <u>Loyalty</u> to a zombie due to either financial dependency on the zombie's resources or a deeper shade of the observer will prevent the zombie from shedding his own shades.

4/22/10—What is this freaking desire to continue! I should have written you three days ago. That's when it all began.

4/19/10—The play is over, I played the part of Jesus Christ. The conflict toward me from the church staff was incredible. I learned a lot. I learned that the only person I need to please is God. One staff member wants to put friends from an ex-ministry in the play to show their clout. Another, let's call him brother doubt, wants to hire his friends to do the technical stuff disregarding my suggestion to use another company but I didn't complained because I know that God can make this thing happen despite the human factor. Long story short the show is done, 12,000 people came to see the play and 430 received and took Christ home with them. You can't tell me that after the entire offering collection is said and done that the show didn't receive some kind of profit production. I get that a lot regarding theatrical productions these days. The person who is collecting the money always seems to say that they came up short. I told my wife something that impressed me the other day. If I were a billionaire and complained about taking a million dollars as a loss, that's one thing but for the person who has nothing and looses all, he is out on the streets. I guess what I'm trying to say is that proclaiming loss is relative to your financial situation. A wealthy mans loss would make a poor man rich.

So what's next did they say. The pastor says 'Fire him', that's right. A suggestion came from another pastor to give me one more chance

to succeed. Take another chance on me and
put me under the supervision of the guy who
wouldn't listen to me regarding what I needed
for the production in the first place. Put me
under the supervision of the one who wanted to
have a reunion on my budget by hiring friends
to perform in the play. By the way I really
don't think you would be to interested in the
things that went wrong about the production
because of too many pastors being involved.
Anyway, like I said the show is over and God
got the glory.

So there I am sweating to complete the demands
of my new supervisor when I get this phone
call. It stops me in my tracks and forces me
to lower my voice. 'Hello—is this Mr. Steven
Sloan'. Yes I reply! This is so & so from
the child support collection agency in Denver
Colorado. We have yet to receive a payment
from you. The last payment we received was
$500 about 9 months ago. I told him that I
didn't understand and I would be home in about
an hour and call him back. I arrived home
about 30 minutes later and concluded my talk
with God along the way. I wanted to know what
the heck was going on. You know the story, for
all I knew my ex-wife had been getting $1000
a month for the past year or so. I instantly
contacted the retirement office and explained
my dilemma. I told them that a child support
collection agency said that they had not been
paid and that I understood that when you retire
that the child support followed you around for
life and into your retirement. They said that
is true. At my retirement they contacted the
controller and the paperwork comes to them
and they deduct it from my retirement pay

each month. The man said he would contact the controller and advise them that they needed the proper paperwork. Can you believe it, since the day I retired not a single child support payment had come out. I just thought that I was being blessed with the money I was getting. I knew that the support payments would not be paid off for 17 years or at age 75 which ever came first. I was really looking forward to getting old so I could see what it would be like free from child support. I found it necessary to explain this situation to my daughter via e-mail due to the fact that it may help cut down and criticism that others may have told her about her dead beat father.

If there was anyway possible to show you the filthy insensitive e-mails she sends me I would love to hear your opinion about her. I'm sure she's a wonderful person to every one who is not her dad. She is, after 30 years, still so very hurt and angry at me for leaving her when she was 3 years old. I just wanted her to know that I was trying to do right with my child support. This time she sent me an e-mail that broke my heart but forget about that, I really was trying to do right. For whatever reason I began to cry. Heavy prayer went from my lips to God as to why this was starting up again. This cry was different, a painful cry, one of those cry's to where if you heard it coming from your neighbors house in the middle of the night you would take the time to get dressed and investigate.

I talked with God in depth. 'Please God—what is going on'. I go to the dedicated prayer room in our house and fall to my knees. I haven't cried like that in a long time. Then it happens. God speaks—'Son, what do you want in life'. I tell Him about the television shows, the plays, the movies, nothing too big. I told Him I thought I was ready to handle it as long as He would be with me through the temptations. He said 'then promise me'. What Lord. 'Promise me that if I give you these things that you will not fall away from me and that I will always be first in your heart'. I told him that I couldn't promise Him because a promise is too easy to break and I am not into breaking promises. He said 'that's why I'm asking you to promise me. You feel so strongly about keeping your promise that you refuse to break it so promise me". I must have fought for another 10 minutes before I gave my word. This time with tears and snot, I made a covenant with the Almighty God himself.

4/20/10—I'm on my way home from work. My cell phone goes off but I can't answer it legally while driving. I pull over to answer to the retirement office. The voice is familiar as being the man who told me that he would contact the City Controller and advise them to send the court ordered child support payment. He advised me that he had spoken with the collection agency in Colorado and had to advise them that there was no court order. At some point after the payments began, the case was reviewed by the Los Angeles City Attorney and found that it was not legitimate. Based on the fact that the child was now almost 30 years old they had canceled the order and therefore did not forward papers to the retirement office to deduct the $1000 monthly payments. I thanked him and was on my way, contemplating the whole situation. After much thanks to God I realized that I had prayed not to be released from my obligation but for justice. Let me now leave this thought with you as I'm very tired and must go to bed but the strangest things are happening to me. When I need to know something, I mean those things that I'm not normally suppose to know—a person will pop up and just tell me the information. It's that way with everything in my life now. I told my wife about the conversation with God and the effects since then. It brought tears to her eyes. I'm telling you, something magnificent happens when God can trust you. There is a scripture at the end of the bible that says that Jesus performed so many miracles that the books cannot contain them. I totally understand that. People are trying to hurt me at the church and God reveals who they are and how to avoid them. Everything I touch turns to my favor, God is revealing everything. Remember the guy who bought the records I recorded 30 years ago, didn't I tell you about that? Quickly—I produced a record in Colorado 30 years ago. I still have several of the original virgin vinyl copies. I meet a record producer who wanted to buy copies. He came to our house tonight from Chicago. I'll tell you about it tomorrow.

7/25/10—Okay—I'm back. Day before yesterday a co-worker comes to me and states that she over heard that I would be terminated on the next day. I thank her and we both agree that this information should have come from my 'I want to protect you' supervisor. On yesterday I am called up to the office where an assistant pastor informs me that the drama department is going to be run by volunteers. In other words my services will no longer be needed. I inquire as to who the volunteers are and they end up be two paid staff personnel who convinced me to leave LAPD in the first place. 'We would like to be able to call on your services in the future'. Heard that line before? It's just a way of saying there is still hope for you so please don't go postal on us. I act excited that there is hope for me to come back in the future, collect severance pay, return the lap top; hand them my keys and walk. What an awesome feeling. It's graduation time. My supervisor sat there requesting that we all meet at the next drama class to tell them about the transition. Deception reigns high in the ministry. With me being present to tell the class about the new paid volunteer taking over would indicate that I agree with it and releases the person taking my place from any back flack or ill feelings that may fall. Use deception to your favor by allowing the shade to believe that you are a bigger one that they. God is so patient with us. Fools lead the church and we reward them with our money. God is the only truth, which leads me to the reason I make this final entry. Without the additional income from the church my wife and I would have never qualified for the purchase of this house. Now that I am released from the deception department, God has an even greater plan. It's not all is lost; it's a promotion to more than I have ever had before. The true test continues with a challenge to my faith. On the day that I was terminated (two days ago) I decided to bar-be-que for my wife. A flash fire occurred and now leaves me in bed with burns over 45% of my body. My blisters itch today and soon I will be healed yet I sit here writing this book talking to true friends and telling them stories of my life. When you here my last words I will start working on a project I filmed for BET film competition. I have my fingers and I have my God and friends. Wait till you see what happens next?

I forgot to tell you—three weeks ago as I was teaching my drama class I told the class that I would be leaving soon and that God was about to promote me.

7/29/10—Entered a film contest last week for BET. The winner gets to produce a $100,000 movie. It's called 'The Stranger Within'; we finished editing this morning and sent off the package today. Yesterday we turndown a job in Vegas due to my burns, feeling better but can't wait to start doing some auditions.

8/5/10—The acting agency says call Rick at 9:35 to see what movie set I will be assigned to as an extra. So I call Rick right on time and the first thing he tells me is that my headshot is not marketable. But fortunate for me he has the number of his photographer friend handy. Is this $150 as big a scam as the lady who told me yesterday that her company will take a picture of me for only $60 and put me on the Internet? At least with the $150 scam I get a disk with three changes and 100 takes. The first scammers put me on a web site that who knows who has the capability to access it. Two thousand dollars left in savings from our tax refund and I taking a shot in the dark. At least Cynthia is in agreement with the idea of making extra money working in films. Don't know if it's true or not but if you're looking to get into the film business don't pay anyone money for working in film unless it's for education or headshot pictures. In about six hours I will have found out if scammer number two has any further problems with me working in the film industry that I need to pay for. Will Steve Sloan get scammed by Rick again in scene II, or will he arrive at a movie set where mysteriously there are no survivors. Hey there's a nice scene for a movie for you—this guy who pays his life savings to be in a movie. He is given directions to an unoccupied warehouse. He is told to deliver his lines and that hidden cameras are focused on wherever he would stand. When he finishes his action he is to go home and wait watching for his film to come out at a theater near you.

8/13/10—The letter came yesterday from EDD. It says I have a credit of $11,700 toward unemployment. Last week I just couldn't let go being led to contact EDD regarding receiving payments even though I was receiving a pension and had a business. I let them know everything. $2000 per month was awarded and is probably exactly what we need to cover our bills but it's only half of what the church took. Get this—day before yesterday not one but two people called from the church and left a message asking if I had certain props they could use for the very pastor who fired me. It was true that I did not have such a prop (electric chair), my only deception was not answering the phone when I saw their names come up on my screen as they were calling. Cindy asks me if we're going to the annual church picnic. Last week we visited an old church in San Bernardino. We were members for years until a very self centered, egotistic minister over music stopped my performance in midstream as I was approaching the stage and I mean I had already began my performance. He felt that my performance would take up too much time and keep one of his many songs from being heard by the multitude. I understand he was fired about a year later for whatever reasons but I just had to go back to see what the ministry was like without him being there to keep people from out shining him. I guess you can tell I'm turning more sinful in my old age but I must admit, that was a growing period in my life. I realized that no matter how hard you work to prepare for God that the enemy can be in the church to stop the process. As long as I work toward God's approval the things that were stopped in the past become the right time in the future. I've done that same performance many times since then www.Youtube/Stevensloan09/Thebullet and it was always well received.

Cindy says let's do the Christmas play on our own, the one our church rejected 'Hand of A Friend'. I think that is a good idea; I'll start working on it and see if we can pick up where we left off. Maybe I can convince all the people who were in the ministry at the time but quit because of the pain of working so hard on the play and getting the boot, maybe they would be willing to work with Cindy and me without the church interfering.

Was that a fiasco or what? Six weeks of rehearsal, over $3000 spent in materials, hours and hours of filming, when the pastor decided to talk to everyone but me, the director, as to how things were coming along. I have reason that even some actor spies may have even fed misinformation to assist in the sedation of the process nevertheless, a lot of people never returned to the church. It's a maturity thing for all of us who desire to use our gifts in the ministry. So—as you can tell by my language that I haven't arrived yet to the epitome of goodness and I guess I never will.

Back to my unemployment check: I Gotta work in the outside world to keep the EDD checks coming in, don't know how that's going to effect production but what else is there in life accept the things that you're called to do. By the way, my answer to my wife about going to the church picnic; I think you can figure that one out.

You figured out why I'm doing this? I mean, why I still write these darn words. It's because I truly believe that God has a plan for my life. I believe that one day the work that I do will be know world wide and with that time comes it would sure be nice for followers to see how it all came to be. I gotta go straighten out this script I'm working on for the Tom Joyner Fantastic Voyage Cruise. Cindy says it's slow so let me put some pep in my step. I'm so glad you spent this time with me. By the way—the new title of this book is 'Don't Work for the Church, Work for God'.

8/30/10—We start filming for the cruise productions tonight, that's the thing I mentioned with Tom Joyner. I kind of like that—Cruise Productions. I wonder if someone is already using that name? Received my first check from EDD unemployment. It's only $450 every two weeks but it's exactly what we need to make ends meet.

8/31/10—Momma says go for it so here we go! I've never seen Cindy so excited to do a production. On tomorrow we will rid ourselves of the remaining savings from the tax return and put it down on the Christmas production 'Hand of A Friend'. I don't know if I told you but this is the play that the church snickered at and requested that I return all the construction materials. Can you imagine the CHURCH making your life a living hell? I guess it happens that way when men are in charge and not God. So I went today to look at the theater in Fontana on Sierra St. I can deal with the small stage.

Still struggling with the flu keeping me from filming for the Tom Joyner Cruise. The actors are hot on my trail asking me how I'm doing. In actor's language that is translated to mean, get healed so we can do some fun stuff! I so appreciate God giving me an understanding wife. I just went on line to look up the price of microphones we need for the play. About $10,000 is what she is asking me to spend in actor's language. We found a place, The Steelworker's Theater in Fontana so here we go.

9/21/10—The unemployment checks continue to come. I look for work while preparing for a December 17th performance of 'Hand of a Friend'. The production for the Tom Joyner cruise was put on Youtube yesterday under Stevensloan09. Now for the fun part, producing myself what the church rejected. My wife is so supportive. If it were up to her this would have happened a year ago.

10-27-10—Publisher called about a week ago. Wanted a copy of this book to see if it's worth printing. What the heck are you talking about! In today economy I could send you spit on a sticky and for the cost of being put on your list of customers you would set me up on the best sellers. So what the heck on top of that I get this letter from the bank that name begins with W.F. they say that the escrow was miscalculated a year ago. Excuse me but we've only been here a year. People are loosing their houses right and left and I'm in the mix. I call them and say I can't afford to pay you $7000 by next month. I'm unemployed. They want proof so I send them my stubs from EDD. Poof—the magic word.

Did you know that If you tell your mortgage company that you are receiving unemployment benefits within the first 90 days. You only have to pay 31% of your total income as the mortgage payment for 6 months. The lady on the phone told me that the down fall is that it really negatively affects your credit. So I say to her 'let's see—roof over our heads, bad credit. Warmth and security—bad credit. About to perform a play that may get us out of debt—bad credit. I called Cindy to tell her that we need to go over this situation tonight after bible study. This is different and I feel eligible for documentation. If I had not been on unemployment I could never have considered paying $1500 instead of $3000 as mortgage. You see you only have to pay 31%

of your income if your receiving unemployment. But that's not what I'm talking about, check this out. My unemployment ends in 6 months. The Bank says if I had not called in within 90 days of being terminated that I would have missed the window to pay half price on my mortgage. Paying half price allows me to save $10,000 by the time unemployment cuts off. This is what I'm saying. What is God going to do in six months that not having unemployment, the mortgage goes back up to $3000 have to do with anything. Watch this folks, you ever wandered what a miracle looks like.

Get your things and come along with me on the ride of my life. I think God I going to put us in warp drive. I forgot to tell you that we're putting on the play Hand of a Friend in December. Ticket sales have already started. Isn't it exciting watching God work? I don't have no job but watch God. I can't pay the mortgage but watch God. My credit is going to pot but watch God, watch!

12/25/10—Been on unemployment for about four months now. I've sent $6000 of the $11,000 allotted to me. The play 'Hand of A Friend' was a flop. So many technical problems—you would not believe. From broken microphones to me forgetting not assigning anyone to the audio board therefore not having actors be heard. Not to mention $20,000 in debt towards my multi million dollar dream play. What was I thinking? The name of this book is now 'Out of Reality and Into Debt' Merry Christmas.

2/18/11—Inspired to document my comfort in the Lord: Since my last entry things have been flowing very smoothly. Just living within our means and receiving unemployment. The play 'Hand of a Friend" didn't pan out very well after all the money we spent. Still other opportunities manifest. The chamber of commerce has been a big inspiration to press forward with our business. A few of the members I convinced to buy tickets came to the performance and had several suggestions. The real reason I'm writing this is because of—o wait a minute I forgot to tell you that my unemployment ran out last week. They say they will automatically resubmit another application. But like I was saying, for the past few days there has been the sweetest comfort in my spirit regarding our finances and the things I should normally be worried about. Whenever I see that things are getting out of my control I realize that I'm not in control and I rest easy at not worrying about what is going to happen. Cindy helps so much by reassuring me that God has a plan for us. I'm currently working on a script for a murder mystery. One of the Chamber members has a nice little restaurant and is acceptable to the idea of a dinner theater. I feel good about it so we're gonna go for it. The Wine Guyz Café is the place and Steve Erickson is on the case. I just wanted to document the blessing before it manifests this time.

2/26/11—A check arrives today, it's from unemployment. My case starts over with a starting balance of $9000. Cindy and I went to a business workshop. Very beneficial, especially the last class of the day. It was regarding labor laws, the instructor suggests that I get a labor law attorney regarding my dismissal from the church. Cindy is checking it out.

3/7/11—I somehow get the impression that this book has somehow turned into a journal. It's been four weeks now and my body is aching. Oh, sorry I forgot to tell you. That church that fired me, they contracted me to build the set for the Easter Production to be held next week and that's why I ache. It's so odd working under these conditions, that is, as an independent contractor. $25 an hour, that's what I charge. By the way, half of the people who called me into the office to fire me, they call me now to tell me how unfair it was that is, now that they have gotten fired, too. I think you know me well enough by now to know my dependence on God to have the utmost say so in my life. Is this not the most perfect situation? I leave as a crippled man, confused and abused, then return in a position above those who caused the pain in the first place. Checks come every week as I hand in my invoices for my services. I've even been asked to switch from set builder to stage manager. Can you say 'we messed up' describes my present source of income by letting me go in the first place? You better believe the stage manager will get paid more than the set builder. They're smart, they want a professional on hand during the program in case something goes array. They may even give me another promotion by asking me to direct the play as close as even one week before the show. And believe you me; the director will make more money than the stage manager. Forgive me if I'm being too direct but church reminds me of the entertainment business. Not to take anything away from God but you could be working for one show one day, fired, then working for another show on the next day. I've learned a great lesson from this experience.

When working for a ministry, use the monetary opportunity to serve God, support your family, pay off your bills and prepare for the sea to close just as soon as you reach the other side of the river. In this day and age you can never put your trust in a job. God is the only thing you can depend on because he is the one who gives you the jobs in the first place. Most people think that working for a church is a most holy position. It can also be the most painful.

How would you like it, not having to worry about loosing your job? Repeat these words! Dear lord Jesus! I know I am a sinner! I believe you died for my sins! Right now, I turn away from my sins and receive you as my personal Lord and savior. Come into my heart, and rule my life. Take away from me the worries of the world and replace it with your love and comfort. In Jesus name, AMEN!

5/28/11—Welcome to the Kingdom of God. I had a meeting with the planning people regarding a building Cynthia and I thought would make us a good theater. It was perfect, sound damping for recording studio, wooden floors for dancing, and huge area for building a stage. The price is only $3000 per month lease. Wait just a minute Steve. What in tar nations is the matter with you? You don't have a job, you're on unemployment, you should be glad you can barely make your mortgage payment.

Yeah I know, isn't it wonderful! When God gets through with this one I'll be ready to write another book on faith and nothing else. By the way—regarding the getting out of debt portion of this book. To this date we have paid nearly $5000 in tithes and offerings for the year. I was called to this building by a friend of mine who himself ventured into it because it was perfect for his needs in business. As he gave me a tour all I could think of was how perfect it would be to have my business there. I stopped coveting my brothers building and went on about my business. Three months later he moved out. By another invitation, not knowing he had moved, I went to that same building only to see a for lease sign out front. After contacting the management he wanted us to get started on the paperwork right away. On the date of this writing the paperwork remains on my desk unsigned. 'If you don't know, go slow' as one preacher so eloquently put it. The planning division for the city of this building is currently checking to see if it is zoned to have students, food and a small theater for production. What I'm trying to say despite whether or not we get the building is that you never know how God will lead you to your true destiny. What or who you are introduced to, may very well be what he had in mind for you, even if it is currently someone else's.

5/12/11—This entry is being made while I am re-reading this manuscript in preparation for publishing. Please forgive all the mistakes you find. I'm a first time book writer. By the way—God did not see fit to give us that building I was telling you about. We've looked at several places to hold our acting classes but the moment we introduce our company to the City Planning divisions they quickly identify us as being in the entertainment industry. All kinds of special permits and charges are quoted. That's perfectly fine with us, after all, did we not ask God to handle the situation and give us the right place for us to have? Gotta get back to page 61 for proofing. If this is the last entry in this book, I'm changing the name of the book to 'God's Way or No Way'. Thank you for taking time to read my life's transitions. Hey! That sounds like a pretty cool title 'Life's Transitions', naaa, I think I'll just stick with the original plan.

CHAPTER 26

BE ANXIOUS FOR NOTHING

05/13/11—At the time of this writing I am reviewing the manuscript for publishing. Got a good deal to publish this book myself. My, how times have changed, I could never have done this when the first pages were written. Anyway—I wanted to tell you about a bad mistake I just made. My wife contributes $1200 every two weeks towards our finances. By the way we have an appointment with Social Security this morning my plan is to duplicate by any means necessary her income so she can retire. She deserves it! Did you know you could collect Social Security while you are working? I am not old enough at this time to collect it along with my retirement but when that time comes (in 5 years) you better believe I will apply. Just the other day on the news they said that Social Security would not exist in another five years. All us baby boomers are taking over the planet. I guess I should quit stalling regarding mistakes I have made, so here's the story. My wife contributes this money by writing me a check from her personal checking account. We do have a joint checking account but I feel it is nice for her to have her own account for fun money. I then take the check on her payday and cash it and put it in the account that is used to pay the bills. Well—mister efficient decides to deposit her check into the account instead of cashing it first and one day ahead of time thinking that it will take at least two days for the check to

arrive at her bank, therefore, all bill paid
on time. On the day after I deposited the check
Cindy gives me a call and says that her bank
notified her that there is a $35.00 bounced
check charge. But I'm quick; I'm slick; I'm
smooth to talk my way out of my stupid, dummy,
finagle butt mistake and I tell her it's okay
because they will run the check again and it
will still cover several bills that would have
cost us even more money if they were not paid
on time.

My plan worked—her voice verifies a since of
comfort. I hang up in a cold sweat and run
to the computer to check the account from
the bills. I'm delayed by a phone call that
ignites my T.V. screen with the words . . .
allow me to stick a pin in this entry for
a moment. Our cable system is such that if
we are watching television and a phone call
comes in, the caller will be announced on
the screen. My transition to my computer is
interrupted by this message that reads 'Los
Angeles Police Department' is on the line.
'It's nothing Steve, probably a friend of yours
from the police station calling to see how you
are doing'. 'Hello—this is the Los Angeles
Police Federal Credit Union, I'm I speaking
with Steven Sloan'? My first instinct was to
change my voice to sound like an animal of some
sort but what kind of example would I be to
you if I were not up front about communicating
with your creditors as one of the rules to
follow while getting out of debt. Be up front
and deal with the situation at hand, then pray
for help. My account has been suspended due
to a check that has bounced. Fourteen other
bills will not get paid and with each one a

$20 check charge. Didn't I learn anything from that guy who wrote that book 'Driving Yourself Out of Debt' had to offer? He clearly said in one of his chapters not to pay the bill until the money was in the bank? Depositing a check with out it first clearing is stupid.

Thankfully, I'm the only human on earth that has ever disobeyed this practice. You can still get into trouble while trying to do right. Okay that's it—I'm done, finished, and kaput, I'm finished with this book. Thank you so much for your patience with me. In fact the new name for this book will be 'Debt—the Never Ending Story'. Naaaa forget it. I'll just keep it the same. I made sure my wife was well informed of the mistake I made and what a fool I was for not being up front with her.

06/03/11—Just 30 more pages away from publishing and I still think about how many times God must have saved my life after reading the events that have occurred over the years. Because of the mistake mentioned above I have gotten us into the worst financial position since we bought the house. Here's the situation. $2200 was deposited into my credit union account from my monthly retirement. I decided to use American Express as our only means of money for the past six weeks. The bill came and I had to pay over $1200 to pay the card off. As you know American Express is due in full at the end of every month. The credit union took out $300 for check charges. Three loans at the credit union are paid automatically once a month, which occurs about a day or two after my retirement money is deposited so that's gone. As you may have guessed, there is about

$500 in my account left and that is where I usually pay the mortgage of $3400.

By the way, I received an email from the credit union yesterday stating that they now need the money. 'What money? You just charged me $300 in overdraft fees'. That's the problem; even though I took the money and paid the checks that bounced the credit union had also paid them. I thought the charges they pinned me with included the amount of the checks. The total came to about $300. That leaves me $200 to apply towards the $3400 mortgage. I still have unemployment coming in it's just that I made a mistake on filling out the bi-weekly form and did not get money for three weeks. Unemployment has been cut from $800 every two weeks to $475 due to the fact that I made $4000 working for the church that fired me during the Easter production. I claimed the $4000 and my allotment from unemployment was reduced. That money should happen on Saturday this weekend. I'm paying all other bills on the day they are due and using credit cards. There is still the comfort that God will prevail. It is without loss of faith that we will be on time with our mortgage due in two weeks but the title of this book is now 'Foreclosure—the Meanest Monster of all'. Maybe I'll continue a second book who knows? At this point it would most likely be about moving into your car after you loose your home. Fair well my friend—thank you for taking the time to listen. THE END—You'll never hear from me again, your friend Steve.

6/5/2011—So what am I going to do about the mortgage payment? I have contacted each credit card for the accurate balance available to me right now. The bills are being paid daily using those credit card accounts. With today being Sunday only one bill is due and I can drive buy and pay it on the way to the theater. Did I tell you I'm playing in The Count o Monte Cristo' for free. Believe me I wouldn't be there if I hadn't given my word. I'm not complaining, maybe what I learning is in God's plan for our new theater.

Things get hectic when you pay a bill on the day its due. I held back from pre paying bills because you are actually assuming you will have the money when you use automatic bill pay from your checking account. It's definitely not a good idea to pay bills using a credit card and is a sure indication that something is wrong with your financial planning. Look at it this way; because of your faithfulness in paying down your credit cards thank God you now have capabilities to get money from another source I call it giving myself a loan even though the interest is torturous. One thing you will quickly learn is that not all bills accept credit cards as a means of payment and if they do you will have to take the time to set up an account for each one individually. You will assign a username and password to each bill you pay by credit card. I have a page in Microsoft Word I use specifically identifying each bill and it's independent usernames and passwords. Be prepared to take a lot of time setting up these accounts. This is dangerous should my computer be hacked they would have all my personal passwords but it's a good thing should my wife need to perform the duties of paying the bills.

Here is my game plan—I'm playing my hand that I can pay off the maxed out credit cards in six months by tightening up our belts being super conscious about our spending other than food and out of the ordinary spending. Remember what got me in this predicament in the first place. That American Express bill for $1200 was out of the ordinary. Though it was for food and pleasure I could have done with about a third of that. The check fees for $350 was out of the ordinary. If only I had listened to my wife and waited to deposit the check one more day. Mistakes on my unemployment forms delayed the timing of $800 income and I'm still waiting for a check. All this because I did not pay attention. That's probably going to be your biggest down fall or failure just before foreclosure. 'Wait a minute! What did he say—I thought this book was about living in your car not a house'.

Didn't I tell you? I changed the name of this book to 'Driving your way to Foreclosure'. By the way I just spoke with a representative from one of the credit cards that stated that I could walk into any bank, present my credit card and walk out with $4200 cash. The interest is 24% there lays the answer to the mortgage payment and we get to keep the house for one more month.

My wife is in the process of reading this manuscript for me so I'll have to step aside but if you're reading this nonsense right now she must have approved it. Look for my next release coming to a bookstore near you. 'Married and Naked on the Streets'. I love you guys! Steve

CHAPTER 27

THE CONCLUSION—REALLY!

8/23/11—Can you believe that all the mistakes and typos you just read still exist even after six proofreading's? Any problems you have found are purely accredited to my ignorance and lack of education. I figured since I was in the neighborhood of the last page that I would drop you a note as to what's happened since my last entry. Let's see now—I have received two more notices from different attorneys regarding the child support that for whatever reason fluctuates up and down at the petitioner's convenience. When I was working for LAPD the amount I owed was $170,000 at $500.00 every two weeks. Miraculously, when I retired now it's $200.00 every two weeks. Prior to that without any job at all it was $200.00 per month.

That doesn't sound like law to me. That has the familiar sound of greed with a capital 'G'. Anyway I'm tire of figures, I'm tired of trying to do it all myself so I'm leaving it up to the Creator and I'm sure He can figure things out regarding the debt thing. People continue to steal from society; more people are in financial trouble than when I first started this book. My wife and I are doing wonderful. I don't mean financially, I think that I've learned that debt will always be a valued part of our lives. I mean that we are happy and love each other and that is probably the most important reality about debt. Owe no man nothing but love (Romans 13:8). Cindy and

I are still believing God for our theater. We still run our little video production company and as long as we continue to pay our tithes God keeps us busy. I start teaching acting classes next month, a local theater has asked me to teach the community acting skills. I've been in two plays and several film auditions. I plan on location scouting to find a place to shoot pictures. I want to show you a picture of me sleeping in the original car I slept in during my mission. That's the front cover and where I am today on the back cover. I guess the real reason for this entry is because I've grown to love you and I really don't want to say good-by. But you know me—I have this strange way of coming back when you least expect it!